Contextualizing the Holodomor

The Impact of Thirty Years
of Ukrainian Famine Studies

Contextualizing the Holodomor

The Impact of Thirty Years of Ukrainian Famine Studies

Edited by Andrij Makuch and Frank E. Sysyn

Canadian Institute of Ukrainian Studies Press
Edmonton   2015   Toronto

Canadian Institute of Ukrainian Studies Press
University of Alberta   University of Toronto
Edmonton, Alberta   Toronto, Ontario
Canada T6G 2H8   Canada M5T 1W5

Copyright © 2015 Canadian Institute of Ukrainian Studies
ISBN 978-1-894865-43-2 (paper)

Library and Archives Canada Cataloguing in Publication

Contextualizing the Holodomor: the impact of thirty years of Ukrainian famine studies / edited by Andrij Makuch and Frank Sysyn.

Includes bibliographical references.
ISBN 978-1-894865-43-2 (paperback)

1. Famines--Ukraine--Congresses. 2. Ukraine--History--Famine, 1932-1933--Congresses. I. Makuch, Andrij, 1956-, editor II. Sysyn, Frank E., editor III. Sysyn, Frank E. Thirty years of research on the Holodomor. IV. Contextualizing the Holodomor: A Conference on the 80th Anniversary (2013: University of Toronto)

DK508.8374.C652015   947.708'4   C2015-903366-7

The printing of this collection was made possible by Ian Ihnatowycz and Marta Witer of Toronto through the Ihnatowycz Family Foundation. We are most grateful for their support.

Cover photo: The first shipment of grain from the "Kakhovka" state farm in the Kherson district, 1930 (courtesy of the Pshenychny Central State Film, Photo, and Sound Archive of Ukraine).

All rights reserved.

No part of this publication may be reproduced, stored in a retrieval system, or transmitted in any form or by any means, electronic, mechanical, photocopying, recording, or otherwise, without the prior permission of the copyright owner.

Printed in Canada

Table of Contents

Preface   vii

**Thirty Years of Research on the Holodomor:
A Balance Sheet**   1
Frank Sysyn

**Towards a Decentred History: The Study of
the Holodomor and Ukrainian Historiography**   14
Olga Andriewsky

**The Impact of Holodomor Studies on
the Understanding of the USSR**   49
Andrea Graziosi

Reflections on Stalin and the Holodomor   76
Françoise Thom

The Holodomor of 1932–33: How and Why?   88
Stanislav Kul'chyts'kyi

**How the Holodomor Can Be Integrated into Our
Understanding of Genocide**   112
Norman M. Naimark

Preface

In 1998 Dr. James Mace inaugurated the Annual Ukrainian Famine Lecture at the University of Toronto. On the occasion of the seventy-fifth anniversary of the Ukrainian Famine, the Toronto Office of the Canadian Institute of Ukrainian Studies, the University of Alberta; the Petro Jacyk Program for the Study of Modern Ukraine of the Centre for European, Russian, and Eurasian Studies of the University of Toronto; and the Ukrainian Canadian Research and Documentation Centre of Toronto held a conference focusing on research and archives in Ukraine and Russia. The conference proceedings were published as a special edition of the *Harriman Review* (Vol. 16, no. 2vii [November 2008]) accessible at http://harriman.columbia.edu/harriman-review and are linked on the website of the Holodomor Research and Education Consortium at http://holodomor.ca/research-and-resources/the-harriman-review.html.

In planning for the eightieth anniversary, the organizing institutions, which now included the Holodomor Research and Educational Consortium (HREC was established in 2013 at the Canadian Institute of Ukrainian Studies through the support of the Temerty Family Foundation) and St. Vladimir Institute, determined that it was appropriate to consider what thirty years of research on the Holodomor had meant for the study of Ukrainian history, Soviet history, genocide, Stalinism, and communism. The conference "Contextualizing the Holodomor: A Conference on the 80th Anniversary" was held at the University of Toronto on September 27–28, 2013. Major funding for this event was provided by HREC through the generosity of James and Louise Temerty and the Temerty Family Foundation, with additional support from the Canadian Foundation for Ukrainian Studies, the Ukrainian Canadian Congress, Toronto branch, and the Ukrainian Studies Fund. The presenters, Olga Andriewsky, Trent University; Andrea Graziosi, University of Naples Federico II; Françoise Thom, Paris-Sorbonne University (Paris IV); Norman Naimark, Stanford University; and Stanislav Kul'chyts'kyi, Institute of History, National Academy of Sciences of Ukraine, addressed the significance of Holodomor studies for one or more of the broader topics. Serving as discussants for the papers were Serhii Plokhy, Harvard University; David Marples, the University of Alberta; Mark von Hagen, Arizona State University; Douglas Irvin, Rutgers University; and Liudmyla Hrynevych, Institute of the History of Ukraine, National Academy of Sciences of Ukraine. Seventeen graduate students and early career scholars from North America and Europe were provided with stipends to support their attendance. The conference concluded with remarks by Roman Serbyn, professor emeritus of Université du Québec à Montréal, who received an award from the Ukrainian Canadian Congress for his many years of research and encouraging study on the Holodomor. The full conference and wide-ranging discussions may be accessed at the HREC website <www.holodomor.ca>.

We are grateful to Oleh S. Ilnytzkyj, editor of the online *East/West: Journal of Ukrainian Studies,* for publishing the conference presentations (Vol. 2, no. 1 [2015]), which now appear here. Andrij Makuch, associate director of research for HREC, undertook the editing of the contributions, with the assistance of Dr. Ilnytzkyj.

The printing of this collection was made possible by Ian Ihnatowycz and Marta Witer of Toronto through the Ihnatowycz Family Foundation. We are most grateful for their support.

Thirty Years of Research on the Holodomor: A Balance Sheet

Frank Sysyn
University of Alberta

Abstract: A background to the articles in this issue, surveying the role of the Harvard Ukrainian Research Institute in the early phase of Holodomor Studies as well as responses to Robert Conquest's *The Harvest of Sorrow: Soviet Collectivization and the Terror-Famine.*

Keywords: Holodomor Studies, Harvard Ukrainian Research Institute, Robert Conquest

In the 1980s the Ukrainian Research Institute at Harvard University (HURI), with which I was then associated, was preoccupied with the Harvard Project in Commemoration of the Millennium of Christianity in Rus'-Ukraine and the Harvard Famine Project, both marking anniversaries (Kohut and Andriewsky 13–16). In the second half of that decade, the thousandth anniversary of the Christianization of Rus'-Ukraine in 1988 engendered a broad agenda of research and publication. The director of HURI, Professor Omeljan Pritsak, and the long-time associate director, Professor Ihor Ševčenko, had already made the Institute and its journal *Harvard Ukrainian Studies* (founded in 1977) leaders in the study of medieval Rus'. They were well disposed to answer the requests of the Ukrainian community and the Ukrainian Studies Fund, which raised funds on behalf of the Institute, that the Institute take an active role in marking this momentous event. At a time when no independent Ukrainian state existed and Ukrainian churches, Catholic and Orthodox, were banned in Ukraine, the marking of the Millennium of the Baptism inevitably had a political dimension. At mid-decade it was clear that the Russian Orthodox Church would centre any commemorations in Moscow, not Kyiv, and that many scholars in the West, not to speak of the media, would treat this event as the Christianization of "Russia." Already in 1984, the Ukrainian Studies Fund began a project to reprint and disseminate scholarly articles dealing with Ukrainian religious and cultural history. Professors Pritsak and Ševčenko conceived a project, beginning in 1987, to publish the original texts and translations of medieval and early modern Ukrainian religious culture in the Harvard Library of Early Ukrainian Literature (20 volumes to date). They also planned an international scholarly congress in Ravenna, Italy in 1988 that resulted in one of the most important publications of papers associated with the commemoration (*Harvard Ukrainian Studies* 12–13 [1988–89]). When the Millennium projects were planned in the mid-1980s, no one could have conceived that by the time of the anniversary, glasnost and perestroika would occur. These changes in the Soviet Union in many ways only sharpened national and religious debates over the significance of the Christianization; they occurred before Ukrainian independence and the restoration of the Ukrainian churches permitted scholars and churchmen in Ukraine to take full part in discussions.

In 1980, as the fiftieth anniversary of the Ukrainian Famine approached, no glimmerings of change in the Soviet Union were in sight. Soviet authorities still denied that any famine had occurred, much less the magnitude of the loss of life it caused. At the same time, the Ukrainian refugees in the West, who were the only group that could bear witness to the tragedy, were aging. I have elsewhere discussed the various projects that put the Ukrainian Famine on the public agenda in North America and Europe in the 1980s, including the film *Harvest of Despair*, the United States Congress Commission on the Ukraine Famine, the International Commission of Inquiry into the 1932–33 Famine in Ukraine, and the first major scholarly conference, held in 1983 in Montreal (Sysyn). Here let me confine myself to the perspective at HURI and the impact of the Harvard Famine Project on the scholarly community.

Until the early 1980s, the Institute had concentrated on medieval and early modern studies, though the Harvard Committee on Ukrainian Studies included the prominent modern history and politics specialists Richard Pipes and Adam Ulam. Then in early 1980 the Ukrainian Studies Fund requested that the Institute mark the anniversary of the Ukrainian Famine in 1982–83 with appropriate scholarly projects. The Ukrainian Famine Project was initiated in 1980, and in 1981 Dr. James Mace, a recent Ph.D. from the University of Michigan, joined the Institute staff to carry on research at Harvard on the Famine. By mid-1981 the Institute, on the recommendation of Adam Ulam, had reached an agreement with Dr. Robert Conquest to write a monograph on the Famine, for which Dr. Mace was to provide major research assistance. The Soviet authorities took note of this activity, and in 1981 a delegation from the U.N. mission of the Ukrainian Soviet Socialist Republic, led by Ivan Khmil' of the Institute of History of the Academy of Sciences of the Ukrainian SSR, paid a visit to the Institute and tried to get it to abandon this project in return for access to Soviet archives and libraries.[1] In 1983 the Institute organized an exhibition on the Famine at Widener Library that was later published in catalogue form (Procyk et al.). James Mace's first article on the Famine appeared in 1984 (Mace), and he and Robert Conquest were among the authors of a booklet titled *The Man-Made Famine in Ukraine*, published by the American Enterprise Institute that year.

The much-anticipated monograph by Robert Conquest, *The Harvest of Sorrow: Soviet Collectivization and the Terror-Famine*, appeared in 1986. The book was sweeping in scope. Conquest dealt with Communist ideology and its relationship to the peasantry before tackling Soviet policies leading up to collectivization and the designation and deportation of kulaks. In emphasizing the role of Stalin, Conquest took a stand in the discussions of the 1980s between the totalitarian school and the revisionists, firmly on the side of the former. Conquest interwove his account with discussions of the nationality issue and religious affairs in the Soviet Union, with special attention to Ukraine. Turning to famine, Conquest wrote one of the first examinations on Central Asia and the mass mortality of the Kazakh Famine of 1931–32. He then discussed the Soviet attack on "Ukrainian nationalism" before turning to the Famine in Ukraine. His graphic depiction of the tragedy used eyewitness testimony. While he confined the use of the term "genocidal" to Ukraine, he also dealt with the famines in the Kuban, the Don region, and the Volga regions, pointing out the large number of Ukrainians and other non-Russian groups there. He used the available evidence to estimate the number of Famine deaths, giving 5 million of 7 million deaths as occurring in Ukraine. He went on to discuss the record of the West in largely not responding to reports of the Famine and, in the case of some reporters, covering it up. Finally he addressed the question of culpability, laying it at the door of Stalin and the regime that had set impossibly high grain requisition quotas and seized foodstuffs, aware that these actions would result in mass starvation—and then tried to cover up the crime. The book had addressed almost all the major issues related to the Famine, interwar Soviet Ukraine, and the Stalinist period. As such it touched on numerous questions and debates in academic as well as political circles.

The book's British (Hutchison) and American (Oxford University Press) publishers and Conquest's renown as a non-fiction writer ensured that the book was reviewed widely, and not only in academic journals. In Canada,

---

[1] This assertion is based on this author's presence at the meeting. Khmil' later discussed the visit and recounted a conversation with James Mace (see Khmil'). His article demonstrates the level of his antagonism to the project, even after he had admitted that the Soviet denial of the Famine was based on falsehoods.

the University of Alberta Press published the book in association with the Canadian Institute of Ukrainian Studies (a list of reviews is appended at the end of this article). No book dealing with Ukraine had ever received such widespread notice. Reviews appeared in *The New York Review of Books, The Times Literary Supplement, The New Republic, Newsweek, Time, The Economist, Foreign Affairs, London Review of Books, Book World Washington Post*, the *Los Angeles Times Book Review, the New York Times Book Review, The Wall Street Journal, The Daily Telegraph, The Sunday Telegraph, The World & I, Policy Review, Commentary, National Review, The Tablet*, and *The Spectator*. The reviewers in these journals generally expressed amazement that a tragedy of this magnitude was unknown to the wider world and that Conquest's book was the first study of the subject. Some such as Michael Bordeaux, eminent churchman and defender of believers in the Soviet bloc, dealt with the moral dimension of the world's indifference to what he saw as a major genocide. While many reviewers called the tragedy genocide, some questioned whether this term was appropriate, especially if they saw Soviet policies as directed against the peasantry and not against Ukrainians per se. But the project had clearly succeeded in bringing the Famine in Ukraine to a vast audience who had little or no inkling of it.

Appearing in 1986, just as glasnost and perestroika were beginning in the Soviet Union, *Harvest of Sorrow* posed a major challenge to the Soviets and their supporters in the West. When the Toronto *Globe and Mail* published two large excerpts from the book (29 November 1986 and 1 December 1986), Yuri Bogayevsky, first secretary at the Soviet embassy in Ottawa, wrote a tortured and convoluted response on 13 December 1986. He insisted that no imposed famine had occurred in 1931–32 (*sic*), though drought conditions had reduced the harvest. He denied that there was mass starvation and dwelled on kulak sabotage in disorganizing agriculture. He asserted that Ukraine's population has remained stable in 1932 and 1933 (32 million) and concluded: "True, times were hard and many people did suffer, especially those families whose fathers, sons, and brothers were murdered by Kulaks. But not nearly to the extent portrayed in less than scholarly publications" (Bogayevsky). Conquest answered this lame response in spirited form in the 10 January 1987 issue ("A drought in Ukraine"). The degree of Soviet consternation over the campaign to promote awareness of the Ukrainian Famine in the West, and Conquest's book in particular, could be seen in the publication of a monograph titled *Fraud, Famine and Fascism. The Ukrainian Genocide Myth from Hitler to Harvard* in 1987 (pages 85-90 deal with Conquest's book). Ostensibly written by Douglas Tottle, a Canadian labour journalist and Communist Party member, the book was likely compiled in the Soviet Union. Certainly its sources, including citations from Ukrainian materials, and its tone of discourse pointed to composition in Kyiv. Reflecting the increasingly untenable nature of the Soviet position on the Famine, the Ukrainian Canadian Communist Kobzar Publishing House had refused the demand of the Communist Party of Canada that it publish the volume. Leading Ukrainian Canadian Communist Peter Krawchuk maintained that the book came recommended by Yurii Kondufor, director of the Institute of History of the Academy of Sciences of the Ukrainian SSR, Academician Arnold Shlepakov, director of the Institute of Social and Economic Problems in Foreign Countries, and Vasyl' Yurchuk, director of the Institute of Party History, a list that, along with the type of research materials presented, points to the book's probable origin (Krawchuk 250).

Scholars of Russian and East European history and Soviet studies and population specialists wrote many of the reviews in general publications (Alec Nove, Geoffrey Hosking, Paul Robert Magocsi, Bruce Lincoln, J. Arch Getty, Peter Wiles, Herbert Ellison) as well as in the more usual academic journals (John A. Armstrong, George Liber, Henry Huttenbach, R. H. Johnston, Stefan Merl, J. Bilocerkowycz, R. E. Johnson, Peter Kenez, Vladimir Brovkin, Gordon B. Smith, L. A. Kosiński, H. Hunter). Academics when writing for broader publics were more likely to be frank in expressing their reactions. The eminent historian of Russia, Geoffrey Hosking, exclaimed in the *Times Literary Supplement*:

> Almost unbelievably, Dr. Conquest's book is the first historical study of what must count as one of the greatest man-made horrors in a century particularly full of them. E. H. Carr used to assert that the history of the Soviet Union after about 1930 probably could not be adequately written, because of the paucity of reliable sources. I had always assumed that this warning applied particularly to the collectivization and especially to the famine; it therefore comes as a shock to discover just how much material has accumulated over the years, most of it perfectly accessible in British libraries..., [and] we are all in Conquest's debt for making coherent what had previously been known in an uncertain and fragmentary way.

Writing in *The New York Review of Books*, the renowned economist and Sovietologist Peter Wiles declared,

> Robert Conquest is one of those rare gifted beings who can combine in one book the results of research, documented and footnotes, with the *haute vulgarisation* thereof. So *The Harvest of Sorrow* is a very good book 'in both kinds' – and let no mere academic say which is more honorable.

He went on to admit that he had always had difficulty in dealing with works such as *The Black Deeds of the Kremlin*, two volumes featuring survivor testimonies published in 1953–55: "I must confess that the title of that book has always put me off from reading it, but it is not the least of Conquest's merits to have ploughed ahead." In this he was joined by Hosking who said: "Western scholars have been inclined to pass snootily by compilations with such lurid titles. But they were wrong; such records represent 'popular history' in a way that ought to appeal to every reader of *Annales*." Wiles asserted that Conquest had espoused the Ukrainian exile view of the Famine and had convinced the reviewer of it. He, like Hosking, accepted the intentionality of the Famine against Ukrainians.

Hosking's and Wiles' reviews reflected the power of Conquest's exposition of what was largely a *terra incognita*, even among specialists of the Soviet Union. Even the sharpest critics of Conquest's book testified to the paucity of scholarly literature.[2] From those who fully accepted Conquest's conclusions to those who rejected major parts of his explanation, scholars grappled with numerous issues raised in the book. Hosking and Wiles had affirmed Conquest's use of survivor testimony, while others were more skeptical of its use as a source. Many reviewers addressed demographic issues, i.e., Conquest's estimate of 5 million deaths in Ukraine and 2 million elsewhere. The noted economist Alec Nove estimated more than 5 million total deaths and saw 7 million in the realm of possibility. Others saw Conquest's estimates as too high. Some questioned his competence and his failure to utilize fully the discussions of S. Rosefielde, S. G. Wheatcroft, R. W. Davis, Barbara Andersen, and Brian Silver on the pages of *Soviet Studies* and *Slavic Review* in the 1980s.[3] Some scholars such as Peter Wiles accepted Conquest's thesis that the origins of the 1932-33 Famine, unlike the Kazakh Famine, could not be found in collectivization. A number of reviewers questioned whether the Famine had been intentional. Others believed that it could not be seen as directed

---

[2] Stephan Merl p. 569 says it had attracted "incredibly little attention" outside of Ukrainian exile literature.

[3] Rosefielde 1980 initiated the discussion. For the other side, see Davies and Wheatcroft 1980 and two articles by Wheatcroft 1981 and 1983. More direct attention to population statistics resulted in further debate that came to be focused more frequently on the Famine: cf. Rosefielde 1983 and 1984; Wheatcroft 1984; Rosefielde 1985; Wheatcroft 1985; also see Anderson and Silver 1985. The latter two authors mention a publication on the Ukrainian Famine to which Mace, Conquest and Dalrymple contributed. This may be seen as an outcome of the Harvard Famine Project, and it discusses the new attention given to the Ukrainian Famine (cf. Anderson and Silver 1985, 518, 532-34). The *Slavic Review* (45.2 [Summer 1986] then published a compendium titled "Ongoing Discussion," which included letters and rejoinders by Robert Conquest, Stephen Cohen, Stephen G. Wheatcroft, Steven Rosefielde, Barbara Anderson and Brian Silver (295-313).

against Ukraine and Ukrainians. The applicability of the term "genocide" was discussed in both general interest and scholarly publications, accepted by many reviewers and contested by others.

Broad as the discussion was, it was not universal, nor always inspiring. Perhaps because so many scholars were writing for wide circulation publications (or because of the book-dispatching policy of the presses), reviews did not appear in some of the most significant professional journals (*Slavic Review, Soviet Studies, Russian Review,* and *Slavonic and East European Review*). The book also became a *casus belli* for some of the revisionist historians, who saw Conquest as a proponent of the totalitarian school, rightist politics, and Ukrainian nationalism. The review by J. Arch Getty in *London Review of Books* may be seen as such an engaged polemical piece. He opined:

> Conquest's hypothesis, sources and evidence are not new. Indeed, he himself first put forward his view two years ago in a work sponsored by the American Enterprise Institute. The intentional famine story, however, has been an article of faith for Ukrainian émigrés in the West since the Cold War. Much of Conquest's most graphic description is taken from such period-pieces as *The Golgotha of Ukraine* (1953), *The Black Deeds of the Kremlin* (1953), and *Communism is the Enemy of Mankind* (1955). Conquest's book will thus give a certain academic credibility to a theory which has not been generally accepted by non-partisan scholars outside the circles of exiled nationalities. In today's conservative political climate, with its 'evil empire' discourse, I am sure the book will be very popular. ("Starving the Ukraine")

Among Conquest's transgressions were that he "even uses Ukrainian place-names rather than their more standardized Russian versions." Getty maintained, "Scholars are obliged to eschew polemic in favour of balanced analysis." Yet for Getty and some of his cohort, balance was difficult to achieve. Some of the most intemperate comments were quoted in a politically partisan piece on the Ukrainian Famine in the *Village Voice*. Roberta Manning of Boston College, described by author Jeff Coplon as a "veteran Sovietologist," is quoted as saying about Conquest: "He's terrible at doing research... He misuses sources, he twists everything" (Coplon 32).

The reception of Conquest's book in 1986–88 could serve as the centerpiece for an examination of the state of the study of Soviet history in the West in the 1980s. But momentous events were quickly overtaking both the Soviet Union and academia. Within a few years, the Soviet Union was no more, scholars from that region could fully take part in international discussions, a wider public there could voice its views, and archives were opened. The emergence of an independent Ukrainian state created a new context for examining the Ukrainian Famine, and thousands and thousands of survivors' testimonies were published. The Soviet denials that a famine or mass deaths had occurred disappeared in the last stages of glasnost. Interpretations could still differ, especially between scholars in Ukraine and Russia, but the internationalization of the study of the Famine to include scholars in these two countries transformed the field. Demographers finally had access to sources that have led to estimates by Oleh Wolowyna and his colleagues of 4 million direct deaths in Ukraine, making Conquest's estimates quite respectable.[4]

We cannot know what would have happened to the academic Ukrainian Famine discussion in the West had the momentous changes not occurred. We can see however that the 1980s marked a watershed in establishing the academic study of the Ukrainian Famine, which since the late 1980s has increasingly been called the Holodomor. The literature on the Holodomor has continued to grow ever since.

WORKS CITED

Anderson, Barbara A. and Brian Silver. "Demographic Analysis and Population Catastrophes in the USSR." *Slavic Review* 44.3 (Autumn 1985): 517–36. Print.

---. "Tautologies in the Study of Excess Mortality in the USSR in the 1930s." *Slavic Review*, 45.2 (Summer, 1986): 307-13. Print.

Bogayevsky, Yuri. "Kulaks Killed Best Workers in Ukraine." *The Globe and Mail* 13 Dec. 1986: D7. Print.

Conquest, Robert. "A Drought in Ukraine." *The Globe and Mail* 10 Jan. 1987: N.pg. Print.

Conquest, Robert, Stephen Cohen and Stephen G. Wheatcroft. [New Demographic Evidence on Excess Collectivization Deaths: Further Comments on Wheatcroft, Rosefielde, Anderson and Silver]. Letter. *Slavic Review* 45.2 (Summer 1986): 295-299. Print.

Coplon, Jeff. "In Search of a Soviet Holocaust: a 55-Year-Old Famine Feeds the Right." *The Village Voice* 12 Jan. 1988: 32. Print.

Davies, R. W. and S. G. Wheatcroft. "Steven Rosefielde's Kliukva." *Slavic Review* 39.4 (Dec. 1980): 593-602. Print.

Getty, J. Arch. "Starving the Ukraine. The Harvest of Sorrow: Soviet Collectivization and the Terror-Famine by Robert Conquest." *London Review of Books* 9.2 (22 Jan. 1987): 7-8. Print.

---

[4] Wolowyna gave the figure in a lecture, "Demographic Complexity of the Holodomor: Beyond the Controversy on the Number of Losses," on 24 November 2014, held at the Canadian Institute of Ukrainian Studies in Edmonton.

The Holodomor of 1932-33. Papers from the 75th Anniversary Conference on the Ukrainian Famine-Genocide, University of Toronto, November 1, 2007. Spec. issue of *The Harriman Review* 16.2 (November 2008). Print.

Hosking, Geoffrey, "Arranging a Catastrophe. Harvest of Sorrow: Soviet Collectivization and the Terror-Famine by Robert Conquest." *TLS – The Times Literary Supplement* 4377 (20 Feb. 1987): 191. Print.

Khmil', Ivan. "Shche odna ialova korova. Pro ideiu stvorennia v Ukraini 'Instytutu Henotsydu.'" *Demokratychna Ukraina* 12 Feb. 1994: N.pg. Print.

Kohut, Zenon E. and Olga A. Andriewsky. "Shaping Ukrainian Studies: A Portrait of Frank E. Sysyn." *Tentorium Honorum: Essays Presented to Frank E. Sysyn on his Sixtieth Birthday.* Ed. Olga Andriewsky et al. Edmonton-Toronto: Canadian Institute of Ukrainian Studies Press, 2010. 1-30. Print.

Krawchuk, Peter. *Our History: The Ukrainian Labour-Farmer Movement in Canada 1907-1991.* Toronto: Lugus, 1996. Print.

Mace, James E. "Famine and Nationalism in Soviet Ukraine." *Problems of Communism* May-June 1984: 37-50. Print.

The Man-Made Famine in Ukraine: Robert Conquest, Dana Darymple, James Mace, Michael Novak. Washington, D.C.: American Enterprise Institute for Public Policy Research, 1984. Print.

Merl, Stephan. "Entfachte Stalin die Hungersnot von 1932-1933 zur Auslöschung des ukrainischen Nationalismus? Anmerkungen zu neueren westlichen Veröffentlichungen über die "ukrainische" Hungersnot." *Jahrbücher für Geschichte Osteuropas* 37.4 (1989): 569-90. Print.

Procyk, Oksana, Leonid Heretz and James E. Mace. *Famine in the Soviet Ukraine 1932-1933: A Memorial Exhibition. Widener Library Harvard University.* Cambridge, MA: Distributed by Harvard UP for Harvard College Library, 1986. Print.

Rosefielde, Steven. "Demographic Analysis and Population Catastrophes in the USSR: A Rejoinder to Barbara Anderson and Brian Silver." *Slavic Review* 45.2 (Summer 1986): 300-06. Print.

---. "Excess Collectivization Deaths, 1929-1933: New Demographic Evidence." *Slavic Review* 43.1 (Spring 1984): 83-88. Print.

---. "Excess Mortality in the Soviet Union: a Reconsideration of the Demographic Consequences of Forced Industrialization, 1929-1949." *Soviet Studies* 35.3 (Jul. 1983): 385-409. Print.

---. "New Demographic Evidence on Collectivization Deaths: a Rejoinder to Stephen Wheatcroft." *Slavic Review* 44.3 (Autumn 1985): 509-16. Print.

---. "The First 'Great Leap Forward.'" *Slavic Review* 39.4 (Dec. 1980): 559-82. Print.

Serbyn, Roman and Bohdan Krawchenko, eds. *Famine in Ukraine, 1932-1933.* Edmonton: Canadian Institute of Ukrainian Studies, 1986. Print.

Silver Brian. "Tautologies in the Study of Excess Mortality in the USSR in the 1930s." *Slavic Review* 45.2 (Summer 1986): 307-13. Print.

Sysyn, Frank E. "The Ukrainian Famine of 1932-33: The Role of the Ukrainian Diaspora in Research and Public Discussion." *Studies in Comparative Genocide.* Ed. Levron Chorbajian and George Shirinian. New York and London: St. Martin's and Macmillan Press, 1999. 182-215. Print.

Tottle, Douglas. *Fraud, Famine and Fascism. The Ukrainian Genocide Myth from Hitler to Harvard.* Toronto: Progress Publishers, 1987. Print.

Wheatcroft, Stephen. G. "A Note on S. Rosefielde's Calculations of Excess Mortality in the USSR, 1929-1949." *Soviet Studies* 36.2 (Apr. 1984): 277-81. Print.

---. "Towards a Thorough Analysis of Soviet Forced Labour Statistics." *Soviet Studies* 35.2 (Apr. 1983): 223-32. Print.

---. "On Assessing the Size of Forced Concentration Labour in the Soviet Union, 1929-1956." *Soviet Studies* 33.2 (Apr. 1981): 265-95. Print.

Wiles, Peter. "The Harvest of Sorrow: Soviet Collectivization and the Terror-Famine by Robert Conquest." *New York Review of Books* 34.5 (26 Mar. 1987): 43-45. Print.

Reviews of *Harvest of Sorrow*

Armstrong, J. A. "The Harvest of Sorrow: Soviet Collectivization and the Terror-Famine by Robert Conquest." *American Historical Review* 92.5 (1987): 1240-41. Print.

Balan, Jars. "History of Horror Keeps Objectivity." *Edmonton Journal* 20 Dec. 1986: F4. Print.

---. "Tottle Review Unscrupulous Twaddle." Letter. *Canadian Dimension* 1987: 2, 46. Print.

Best, Paul J. "The Harvest of Sorrow: Soviet Collectivization and the Terror Famine by Robert Conquest." *The Polish Review* 35.3/4 (1990): 185-88. Print.

Bilocerkowycz, J. "The Harvest of Sorrow: Soviet Collectivization and the Terror-Famine by Robert Conquest." *Problems of Communism* 38.4 (1989): 133-40. Print.

Blake, Patricia. "Books: The War Against the Peasants the Harvest of Sorrow by Robert Conquest." *Time* 8 Dec. 1986: 91-92. Print.

Booker, Christopher. "A Mad Avalanche of Evil. The Harvest of Sorrow: Soviet Collectivization and the Terror-Famine by Robert Conquest." *The Spectator* 25 Oct. 1986: 32-34. Print.

Bourdeaux, Michael. "The Harvest of Sorrow: Soviet Collectivization and the Terror-Famine by Robert Conquest." *Church Times* 21 Nov. 1986: 6. Print.

Brovkin, Vladimir N. "Robert Conquest's *Harvest of Sorrow*: a Challenge to the Revisionists." *Harvard Ukrainian Studies* 11.1/2 (June 1987): 234-45. Print.

Campbell, John C. "The Harvest of Sorrow: Soviet Collectivization and the Terror-Famine by Robert Conquest. Famine in the Ukraine, 1932-1933." Ed. Roman Serbyn and Bohdan Krawchenko. *Foreign Affairs* 65.4 (Spring, 1987): 908. Print.

Conquest, Robert. "Harvest of Sorrow." Letter. *The New Republic* 1 Dec. 1986: 3. Print.

---. Reply to Letter of J. Arch Getty. *London Review of Books* 9.9 7 May 1987. http://www.lrb.co.uk/v09/n02/j-arch-getty/starving-the-ukraine. Web.

---. Reply to Letter of J. Arch Getty. *London Review of Books* 9.17. 1 Oct. 1987. http://www.lrb.co.uk/v09/n02/j-arch-getty/starving-the-ukraine. Web.

"Conquest's "Harvest of Sorrow": an Overview of the Reviews." *The Ukrainian Weekly* 25 Jan. 1987. 5, 12. Print.

Davies, R. W. "Reviews: The Harvest of Sorrow: Soviet Collectivization and the Terror-Famine by Robert Conquest." *Detente* 9/10 (1987): 44-45. Print.
Ellison, Herbert J. "Harvest of Sorrow: Soviet Collectivization and the Terror-Famine by Robert Conquest." *The Los Angeles Times* 19 Nov. 1986: 1-2. Print.
Ennew, C. "The Harvest of Sorrow: Soviet Collectivization and the Terror-Famine by Robert Conquest." *Journal of Agricultural Economics* 38.3 (1987): 521-22. Print.
Floyd, David. "Man-made famine." *The Daily Telegraph* 12 Sep. 1986. N.pg. Print.
"Genocide in the Ukraine." *The Economist* 11 Oct. 1986: 104. Print.
Getty, J. Arch. "Starving the Ukraine. The Harvest of Sorrow: Soviet Collectivization and the Terror-Famine by Robert Conquest." *London Review of Books* 9.2 (22 Jan. 1987): 7-8. Print. [See also letters between Robert Conquest and J. Arch Getty.]
---. Reply to Letter of Robert Conquest. *London Review of Books* 9.10 21 May 1987. http://www.lrb.co.uk/v09/n02/j-arch-getty/starving-the-ukraine. Web.
---. Reply to Letter of Robert Conquest. *London Review of Books* 9.19 20 Oct. 1987. http://www.lrb.co.uk/v09/n02/j-arch-getty/starving-the-ukraine. Web.
Goodman, Walter. "Putting Pieces Together For Soviet Famine Book. Scholar Studies 'Things I Want To Know About.'" *The New York Times* 15 Oct. 1986. 86D. Print.
Gross, John. "Review of the Harvest of Sorrow." *The New York Times* 7 Oct. 1986: C17. Print.
"The Harvest of Sorrow: Soviet Collectivization and the Terror-Famine by Robert Conquest." *The Wilson Quarterly* 11.1 (1987): 155-6. Print.
Heller, M. "The Harvest of Sorrow: Soviet Collectivization and the Terror-Famine by Robert Conquest." *Quinzaine Litteraire* 479 (1987): 23. Print.
Hillier, Bevis. "'Harvest' of Soviet Terrorism Reaped by Historian Conquest." *The Los Angeles Times* 19 Nov. 1986: 1-2. Print.
Hosking, Geoffrey, "Arranging a Catastrophe. Harvest of Sorrow: Soviet Collectivization and the Terror-Famine by Robert Conquest." *TLS – The Times Literary Supplement* 4377 (20 Feb. 1987): 191. Print.
Hunter, Holland. "The Harvest of Sorrow: Soviet Collectivization and the Terror-Famine by Robert Conquest." *Annals of the American Academy of Political and Social Science* 496 (March 1988): 152. Print.
Huttenbach, Henry. "The Harvest of Sorrow: Soviet Collectivization and the Terror-Famine by Robert Conquest." *Martyrdom and Resistance* 13.4 (March-April 1987): 1, 10. Print.
Johnson, R. E. "The Harvest of Sorrow: Soviet Collectivization and the Terror-Famine by Robert Conquest." *Labour / Le Travail* 23 (1989): 379-81. Print.
Johnston, R. H. "Robert Conquest. The Harvest of Sorrow: Soviet Collectivization and the Terror-Famine." *Canadian Slavonic Papers / Revue Canadienne Des Slavistes* 29.2/3 (June-September 1987): 348-49. Print.
Kenez, Peter. "The Harvest of Sorrow: Soviet Collectivization and the Terror-Famine by Robert Conquest." *Society* 25.3 (1988): 94-96. Print.
Kosiński, L. A. "The Harvest of Sorrow: Soviet Collectivization and the Terror-Famine by Robert Conquest." *Population and Development Review* 13.1 (March 1987): 149-53. Print.
Lawrence, John. "Ukrainian Genocide." *The Tablet* 1 Nov. 1986: 4. Print.

Liber, George. "The Harvest of Sorrow: Soviet Collectivization and the Terror-Famine by Robert Conquest." *Political Science Quarterly* 103.2 (1988): 400-01. Print.

Lieven, Anatol. "Ukrainian Genocide." *The Tablet* 22 Nov. 1986. http://archive.thetablet.co.uk/article/22nd-november-1986/14/ukrainian-genocide. Web.

Lincoln, Bruce. "Russia's Grim Famine History." *The World & I* Apr. 1987: 424-30. Print.

Magocsi, Paul Robert. "Famine or Genocide." *The World & I* Apr. 1987: 416-23. Print.

Meissner, Frank. "The high price of Soviet agricultural collectivization: The Harvest of Sorrow: Soviet Collectivization and the Terror-Famine by Robert Conquest." *Food Policy* 12.4 1987: 403-05. Print.

Merl, Stephan. "Entfachte Stalin die Hungersnot von 1932-1933 zur Auslöschung des ukrainischen Nationalismus? Anmerkungen zu neueren westlichen Veröffentlichungen über die "ukrainische" Hungersnot." *Jahrbücher für Geschichte Osteuropas* 37.4 (1989): 569-90. Print.

---. "Wie viele Opfer forderte die "Liquidierung der Kulaken als Klasse"? Anmerkungen zu einem Buch von Robert Conquest." *Geschichte und Gesellschaft* 14.4 (1988): 534-40. Web.

Methvin, Eugene H. "The Other Holocaust." *National Review* 39.3 28 Feb. 1987: 48-49. Print.

Miller, Jim. "The Grim Hunger." *Newsweek* 17 Nov. 1986: 95. Print.

Mount, Ferdinand. "Ruling Through Famine." *The Sunday Telegraph* 28 Sep. 1986: 14. Print.

Neilson, K. "The Harvest of Sorrow: Soviet Collectivization and the Terror-Famine by Robert Conquest." *Queens Quarterly* 5.1 (1988): 193-96. Print.

Nove, Alec. "When the Head Is Off...The Harvest of Sorrow: Soviet Collectivization and the Terror-Famine by Robert Conquest." *The New Republic* 195.18 (3 Nov. 1986): 34-7. Print.

Prager, Dennis. "The moral riddle of our time. Why don't all good people hate Communism?" *Ultimate Issues* 2.4 (Fall 1986): 1-6. Print.

Puddington, Arch. "The Harvest of Sorrow: Soviet Collectivization and the Terror-Famine by Robert Conquest." *Commentary* 83.6 (1 Jun. 1987): 74-7. Print.

"Robert Conquest." *Queens Quarterly* 5.1 (1988): 193-96. Print.

Salisbury, Arnold. "The Ukrainian Holocaust Documented." *Global Affairs* (Spring 1987): N.pg. Print.

---. "The Ukrainian Holocaust Documented." *The New York City Tribune* 20 Apr. 1987: N.pg. Print.

Shannon, William V. "The wounds from the past that thwart Gorbachev's reform plans." *The Boston Globe* 11 Feb. 1987: 15. Print.

Simes, Dmitri K. "Stalin and His War Against the Peasantry." *Book World; The Washington Post* 16.42 (19 Oct. 1986): 3, 14. Print.

Smith, Gordon. B. "The Harvest of Sorrow: Soviet Collectivization and the Terror-Famine by Robert Conquest." *The Journal of Politics* 49.3 (August 1987): 904-05. Print.

Sorokowski, Andrew. "Ukrainian Genocide." *The Tablet* 6 Dec. 1986: 12. Print.

"Terror beyond belief. Robert Conquest on how Soviet and Western experts are coming to terms with the extent of Stalin's purges." *The Independent* 12 May 1988: N.pg. Print.

Thomas, K. T. "The Harvest of Sorrow: Soviet Collectivization and the Terror-Famine by Robert Conquest." *Radical History Review* 52 (1992): 121-31. Print.

Tottle, Douglas. "The Realm of Subjectivity." *Canadian Dimension* March 1987: 36-37. Print.

Warren, Spencer. "The Harvest of Sorrow: Soviet Collectivization and the Terror-Famine by Robert Conquest." *Policy Review* 39 (1987): 84-5. Print.

Whitney, Craig. "The Harvest of Sorrow: Soviet Collectivization and the Terror-Famine by Robert Conquest." *The New York Times Book Review* 26 Oct. 1986: 11-12. Print.

Wiles, Peter. "The Harvest of Sorrow: Soviet Collectivization and the Terror-Famine by Robert Conquest." *New York Review of Books* 34.5 (26 Mar. 1987): 43-45. Print.

Will, George F. "Stalin's Right-Hand Man." *The Washington Post* 16 Nov. 1986: K7. Print.

"Zhnyva Pechali." *Ukrains'ki visti* (Detroit) 23 Nov. 1986: 2-4. Print.

Towards a Decentred History: The Study of the Holodomor and Ukrainian Historiography

Olga Andriewsky
Trent University

Abstract: This article reviews research on the Holodomor by historians of Ukraine since the late 1980s. It examines the dominant trends in historiography, the major findings, and the current state of the field. The field itself, it argues, has grown considerably and there now exists a critical body of scholarship on the subject. For the past two decades, this scholarship has largely been dominated by the debate about whether the Holodomor constitutes genocide. Much of the focus has been on illuminating the policies, methods, and intentions of the Soviet leadership and there have been notable advances in these areas of research. Social history on this topic, on the other hand, remains largely underdeveloped. Some historians of Ukraine have begun to study the Holodomor "from below" and to explore the larger social and cultural consequences of de-kulakization, collectivization, and the Terror-Famine. This approach is crucial, the author suggests, to understanding the exceptional nature of the era. In terms of patterns of migration, family structure, religious practices, social identity, status and ranking, and attitudes towards power, authority, and political participation, the Holodomor era fundamentally changed the way Ukrainians lived. In this respect, it represents a turning point, as momentous as perhaps any in Ukrainian history.

Keywords: Famine, Ukrainian historiography, Genocide, Stalin

Long before scholars in the Soviet Union and the West turned their attention to the subject of the Famine of 1932–33 in Ukraine, there was an audience anxious for the story to be told. Indeed, survivors in Canada and the United States, and elsewhere, did not simply wait passively for historians to begin studying what had happened to them in Ukraine under Stalin. They began recording their experiences decades before Robert Conquest's landmark study, *The Harvest of Sorrow*, was published in 1986 (see also Suslyk; Solovey). In the 1950s, for example, a group of survivors in the diaspora published two volumes of memoirs and eyewitness accounts entitled *The Black Deeds of the Kremlin* (see Pidhainy). In fact, the Ukrainian diaspora played an active role not only in attempting to publicize the Holodomor but also in supporting research in North America, especially, the Harvard Famine Project of the 1980s, with which both Robert Conquest and James Mace were at one time associated (Sysyn 187–90).

Similarly, in Ukraine, it was "pressure from below" that in the late 1980s broke more than a half-century of official silence on the subject. In 1988, as Stanislav Kul'chyts'kyi and others have noted, it was Ukrainian writers—Oleksii Musiienko, Ivan Drach, Borys Oliinyk, and Yurii Shcherbak—who first raised in public the issue of the deaths of millions of Ukrainians in the famine of the early 1930s (Kulchytsky, "Why Did Stalin"). (The writer and civic activist Ivan Drach is usually credited with popularizing the term "*holodomor*"—meaning "extermination by hunger"—from *moryty holodom*.) Moreover, beginning in 1989, throughout Ukraine, in Poltava, Kharkiv, Kyiv, Vinnytsia, Zhytomyr, Dnipropetrovsk, and Luhansk oblasts, as the historian Oleksandra Veselova has described, memorials to the victims began to appear spontaneously in villages and towns, often in the form of crosses at the sites of known mass graves or at locations where churches had stood and were subsequently destroyed in the 1930s (Veselova, "Pam'iatni znaky"). By the summer of 1991, two journalists, Volodymyr Maniak and Lidiia Kovalenko, had published the first major book of interviews with survivors in Ukraine, "*33-i Holod": Narodna knyha—Memorial* (see Maniak and Kovalenko). The Holodomor, in this respect, has never been just an academic subject.

Indeed, as much as historians like to lament the politicization of scholarship on the subject, there has *always* been a political dimension to the study of the Holodomor. "Everything is political by the nature of things," Michel Foucault reminds us. "Everything is political by the existence of adversaries" (Foucault 390). From the half-century-long suppression of any public mention of the Famine in the Soviet Union to the creation of the U.S. Commission on the Ukraine Famine under President Ronald Reagan in 1986, the study of the Holodomor has been enmeshed in a larger political discourse on the Soviet Union. It is a matter in which many different institutional and non-institutional actors have had and continue to have a vital stake. The interpretation of the Holodomor remains an especially contentious issue in relations between Russia and Ukraine.[1]

The peculiar dynamics of Holodomor Studies notwithstanding, the primary aim of this essay is to examine the research that has been done on the subject by historians of Ukraine over the course of the last three decades. What have historians of Ukraine learned about the Holodomor? What are the trends in Ukrainian historiography? How has our

---

[1] As several U.S. State Department cables published in *WikiLeaks* attest, Russian diplomatic officials began actively working to "discourage" the international recognition of the Holodomor as genocide in 2008. See Zawada. See also Kul'chyts'kyi, "Vynyshchuval'ni aktsii"; and Verstiuk.

understanding of the Terror-Famine changed? How has our understanding of Ukrainian history changed as a result?[2] It is not my intention—it should be noted at the outset—to discuss popular conceptions and representations of the Holodomor. The politics of Holodomor commemoration are also not a main focus here. These are separate and complex topics that merit serious attention in their own right.[3] I would, however, like to return—briefly—to the politics of Holodomor Studies in order to provide some context to understanding the course of research, research funding, and publication in recent years.

THE POLITICS OF HOLODOMOR STUDIES: A FEW WORDS

There has been a profound transformation in the study of the Holodomor since the late 1980s. Perhaps, more accurately, it is the world in which the Holodomor is studied that has changed. The Soviet Union no longer exists. The archives in Ukraine and Russia became accessible in the late 1980s and early 1990s (though that trend has been to some degree reversed, particularly in Russia). The centre of research itself has moved from North America to Ukraine.

In the last decade, moreover, there has been a series of dramatic shifts in official policy and attitudes towards the Holodomor in Ukraine. Between 1991 and 2010, every president of Ukraine, beginning with Leonid Kravchuk, lent his support to the study of the Holodomor. Kravchuk was, in fact, the first president to refer to the Holodomor as genocide (Kravchuk 10).[4] Under President Viktor Yushchenko, who came to power in 2005 in the wake of the pro-Western Orange Revolution, however, the public

---

[2] By "Ukrainian historiography" I mean the work of professional historians who focus on the history of Ukraine, not the Soviet Union at large. To be sure, the boundaries between what constitutes Soviet history and Ukrainian history can be quite blurred and often overlap. The works of Hiroaki Kuromiya, Terry Martin, and Lynne Viola, for example, have much to say about Ukraine and the workings of the Soviet Union at large.

[3] The politics of Holodomor commemoration can, by now, be considered a sub-specialty of the field. See, for example, Soldatenko, "Trahediia trydtsiat' tret'oho"; Himka; Viedienieiev and Budkov; Kas'ianov; Boryk; and Motyl.

[4] In 1993, at a conference in Kyiv on the 60th anniversary of the Holodomor, Leonid Kravchuk, the first president of Ukraine in the post-Soviet era, remarked: "I agree completely that this was a planned action and that this was a genocide committed against the people. But we can't stop there. Yes, it was against the people, but it was directed from a different centre. That is how this horrendous page of our history should be treated."

commemoration and study of the Holodomor became a major state project. (Yushchenko himself was born and grew up in a Ukrainian village in Sumy oblast—one of the hardest hit regions in Ukraine during the Terror-Famine.)

What was unusual after 2005 was the unprecedented scale of effort. Yushchenko launched an ambitious, nationwide program of education, research and documentation, and commemoration. The fourth Saturday of November was designated by presidential decree as an official day of remembrance for "the victims of the Holodomors (*sic*)" (Ukaz Prezydenta Ukrainy № 431/2007).[5] [Note the use of the plural here. The victims of the famines of 1921–22 and 1946–47 were included in the commemorations as well.] On 28 November 2006, the Parliament of Ukraine, with the president's support and in consultation with the National Academy of Sciences, voted to recognize the Ukrainian Famine of 1932–33 as a deliberate act of genocide against the Ukrainian people ("Zakon Ukrainy pro Holodomor"). A vigorous international campaign was subsequently initiated by the Ministry of Foreign Affairs to have the United Nations, the Council of Europe, and other governments do the same.

Under Yushchenko, academic research and public education received considerable attention and unparalleled support. A museum in memory of the "Victims of the Holodomors" (*Natsional'nyi muzei "Memorial pam'iati zhertv Holodomoriv v Ukraini*) was constructed in Kyiv for the 75th anniversary in 2008. Built on a hill overlooking the Monastery of the Caves and the Dnipro River—one of the most sacred sites in all of Ukraine—the museum houses a permanent exhibit and a Hall of Memory (reminiscent of the Hall of Remembrance at the U.S. Holocaust Museum in Washington), where visitors can light a candle and ring a bell in memory of victims. To promote public awareness, the teaching of the Holodomor was introduced in schools throughout Ukraine, including post-secondary institutions and military schools. Provisions were made for the development of curricula and educational materials. National essay writing contests were organized for students at all levels of the school system ("Ukaz Prezydenta Ukrainy № 431/2007").

In 2006, as part of the project, the Ukrainian Institute of National Memory (*Ukrains'kyi institut natsional'noi pam'iati*) was established directly

---

[5] It was President Kuchma who in 1998 originally designated the fourth Saturday of November as a day to commemorate "the victims of the Holodomors (*sic*) and political repression" ("Ukaz Prezydenta Ukrainy № 1310/98"). Yushchenko, in 2007, assigned a separate day in May for the victims of political repression—thus elevating the symbolic significance of the Holodomor(s).

under presidential administration. The mandate of the Institute was to conduct research and promote "the public memory of Ukrainian history with special attention to the twentieth century, the national liberation struggles, and the victims of "the Holodomors" and political repression." In particular, the Institute was given the task of organizing a "National Book of Memory" (*Natsional'na Knyha pam'iati*) in preparation for the 75th anniversary of the Terror-Famine in 2008. The *National Book of Memory* consists of nineteen volumes, a general volume as well as one volume for each of the seventeen oblasts/regions affected by the Holodomor. There is a separate volume on the city of Kyiv. Regional volumes were prepared by the respective oblast administration using a predetermined template. Thus, each regional volume includes an introductory article by a local historian, documents relating to events in the region, eyewitness testimony, photographs, newspaper accounts as well as the names of Holodomor victims. To date, researchers have identified the names of some 882,510 victims of the Ukrainian Famine of 1932-33.[6] President Yushchenko himself wrote the introduction to the main volume, referring to the Holodomor of 1932-33 as genocide, "the greatest tragedy in the history of the Ukrainian people" (vol. 1, 7). The *National Book of Memory* was a remarkably ambitious series completed in an astonishingly short period of time.

In general, under Yushchenko, research and publications on the Holodomor increased significantly. In 2007-2008, the high point of activity, over 250 academic books, articles, and collections of documents were published according to the former Director of the Institute of National Memory (Soldatenko "Trahediia" 9). The Yushchenko presidency was, in this respect, a "tipping point" in the study and popularization of the Holodomor. According to polling done in Ukraine in November 2013, 66 percent of the population of Ukraine regarded the Holodomor as genocide, and that percentage continues to rise (22 percent rejected the idea, 12 percent had no opinion) ("Dvi tretyny").[7]

---

[6] There have been questions raised about the accuracy of the lists of victims. See Soldatenko, "Trahediia" 43-45. Given the time constraints that researchers were working under and the difficulty of recovering this kind of information many generations after the fact, errors and omissions would seem natural, indeed, inevitable.

[7] There are of course, marked regional differences. Support was lowest in Crimea and the Donbas. What is often overlooked, however, is the rural/urban difference: 79 percent of the rural population is convinced that the Holodomor was genocide as compared to 60 percent of the urban population. See also "Kil'kist' ukraintsiv" and "Polovyna zhyteliv."

In 2010, when Viktor Yanukovych, the leader of the pro-Russian Party of Regions, became president of Ukraine, the Holodomor was quickly demoted in terms of its official and symbolic importance (Motyl, "Deleting the Holodomor"). In April 2010, just as the Parliamentary Assembly of the Council of Europe was about to consider a resolution recognizing the Holodomor as genocide of the Ukrainian people (a Yushchenko initiative), President Yanukovych reversed Ukraine's official position. In Strasbourg, in an astonishing about-face, he declared, "We consider it incorrect and unjust to consider the Holodomor a fact of genocide of a certain people." It was, he said, "a common tragedy" of the Soviet people, claiming the lives of Russians, Belarusians, and Kazakhs as well as Ukrainians. "Those were the consequences of Stalin's totalitarian regime, his attitude to people," he said ("Yanukovych Reverses").

President Yanukovych's position on the Holodomor had immediate repercussions in academic circles. In July 2010, he appointed Valerii Soldatenko, a historian and member of the Communist Party of Ukraine, as head of the Institute of National Memory to replace Ihor Iukhnovs'kyi, the prominent physicist, parliamentarian, and a member of Yushchenko's party, Our Ukraine. In fact, the entire administration and staff of the Institute were eventually relieved of duties ("Iz Instituta Natspam'iati"). In one of his first public interviews, the newly appointed director explained his views on the Holodomor, echoing the point that Yanukovych had made at the Council of Europe that the 1932–33 famine in Ukraine was "a terrible tragedy," "the result of difficult circumstances," but not deliberate. He also made clear that he prefers the term *holod* ("famine") rather than *Holodomor* ("Communist Ukrainian"). In response to Soldatenko's appointment, a group of prominent intellectuals, including several historians associated with the Institute of National Memory under Iukhnovs'kyi, created the "Public Committee to Honour the Memory of the Victims of the Holodomor-Genocide" (*Holodomor 1932–1933*).

Under Soldatenko, the Institute of National Memory shifted its focus away from researching the Holodomor to other eras of Ukrainian history, most notably, the Cossack period and the Second World War. On the eightieth anniversary of the Famine in 2013, for example, the Institute of National Memory played a negligible role in marking the event. Perhaps most sensationally, the deputy director of the Institute, Dmytro Viedienieiev co-authored *Zaruchnytsia hlobal'noho protystoiannia: Trahediia Velykoho Holodu 1932–1933 rr. v Ukraini v konteksti "kholodnoi viiny" (1945–1991 rr.)* [Hostage of Global Confrontation: The Tragedy of the Great Famine of 1932–33 in Ukraine in the Context of the "Cold War"]. Tendentious and, in many ways, reminiscent of Soviet-era publications, the book argued that the Holodomor was a political project promoted by U.S. intelligence, American

Sovietologists, and "Ukrainian nationalists" in the diaspora over the course of many decades—part of a deliberate campaign of psychological warfare waged against the Soviet Union.[8] On 25 November 2013, the Institute sponsored a round-table discussion on this topic—the politics of memory—with the participation of Viedienieiev, the historian Heorhii Kas'ianov, and Viktor Voronin, an archivist (Soldatenko, "Ukrains'kyi instytut" 2). The study of the Holodomor, in line with Yanukovych's own position on the subject, was thus reduced in importance by the officially appointed keepers of "national memory."

Predictably, with the fall of Yanukovych, the Institute of National Memory has once again changed course. In March 2014, Volodymyr V'iatrovych, a thirty-seven-year-old historian, former director of the Archives of the Security Service of Ukraine, and member of the "Public Committee to Honour the Memory of the Victims of the Holodomor-Genocide" was appointed as the new director of the Institute of National Memory ("Vitse-prem'ier"). V'iatrovych's views on the Terror-Famine are well known—he is an active proponent of the concept of the Holodomor as genocide. Whether research on the Holodomor once again becomes a national priority in its own right—with targeted funding—remains to be seen. Much depends, of course, on how events in Ukraine continue to unfold.

What Have We Learned?

Let us now return to our main questions—what have historians of Ukraine learned about the Holodomor? How has the scholarly work on the Ukrainian Famine done over the last 30 years added or changed their understanding? What are the trends in historiography?

Thirty years ago, it was possible to count the number of scholars working on some aspect of the Terror-Famine of 1932–33 on the fingers of one hand—Robert Conquest, James Mace, Roman Serbyn, Marco Carynnyk, and the demographer Sergei Maksudov. When, in 1983, Roman Serbyn organized a scholarly conference on the Famine of 1932–33 at the University of Montreal, it was a historic event in its own right. (The

---

[8] The problem with this argument is that the Holodomor did not become part of the Cold War discourse in the U.S. until the mid-1980s and, even then, remained well on the margins of political and scholarly discussion. The authors appear unaware of what Frank Sysyn has called the great "inattention" of Western scholarship to this subject between the 1930s and 1980s. On the lack of interest in the Terror-Famine among Sovietologists and the intelligence community in the early years of the Cold War, see Andriewsky and Pringle.

proceedings were subsequently published in 1986 by the Canadian Institute of Ukrainian Studies as *Famine in Ukraine 1932–1933*; see Serbyn and Krawchenko). After the publication of Robert Conquest's book in 1986, James Mace remained the *only* historian in the United States researching the Famine. He first served as research assistant to Robert Conquest on *Harvest of Sorrow* while at the Harvard Ukrainian Research Institute. Then, in 1986 just as Conquest's book was going to print, he was appointed the Staff Director of the U.S. Commission on the Ukraine Famine in Washington.

James Mace was the first and, for a very long time, the only historian to go on record stating that the famine of 1932–33 in Ukraine constituted genocide (United States Commission xxiii). Not even Robert Conquest had gone quite that far. Without access to archival materials, without some knowledge of what was going on behind the scenes, few historians were willing to risk their credibility in making definitive pronouncements about the intentions of the Soviet leadership.[9]

Thirty years later, historians of Ukraine are no longer trying to convince their colleagues, as they were in the 1980s, that the death of millions of people in 1932–33 in Ukraine merits serious study. Today, there is a substantial cohort of professional historians engaged in original research, in exploring various aspects of the Holodomor. There is a large and growing list of publications. By some estimates, there are now over 20,000 publications relating to the Holodomor, the great majority of these appearing after the year 2000 (cf. the opening statements of the article by Stanislav Kul'chyts'kyi in this volume). We now have more than four thousand interviews with Holodomor survivors. Over 250 collections of documents have been assembled and published in Ukraine (Soldatenko, "Trahediia" 8–11; Botushans'ka). Archival collections have been catalogued and guides to these collections have been made public (Boriak and Papakin). There is, by now, a critical body of scholarship on the subject.

And even opponents of the concept of the Holodomor as genocide now concede that this has become the standard historical narrative in Ukraine (Soldatenko, "Trahediia" 4–8). The widespread use of the term Holodomor—rather than "famine"—is one sign of how much has changed. For most historians of Ukraine, and, indeed many non-historians, the word

---

[9] Much of the early research in Canada and the United States in the 1980s tended to concentrate on foreign diplomatic and press accounts of the famine, on what British and American journalists and diplomats knew, because these sources were accessible (See Carynnyk).

"famine" no longer seems adequate to describe what happened in Ukraine in 1932–33.[10]

Indeed, in retrospect, it is remarkable how well James Mace's conclusions, stated in the U.S. Commission's Report to Congress in April 1988, have held up over time. Working with the official Soviet press and other published Soviet sources, with reports by Western journalists and diplomatic records, as well as with survivor accounts—but with no access to Soviet archives—he provided a remarkably cogent analysis. The Commission arrived at the following conclusions (vi-vii):[11]

1. There is no doubt that large numbers of inhabitants of the Ukrainian SSR and the North Caucasus Territory starved to death in a man-made famine in 1932–1933, caused by the seizure of the 1932 crop by Soviet authorities.
2. The victims of the Ukrainian Famine numbered in the millions.
3. Official Soviet allegations of "kulak sabotage," upon which all "difficulties" were blamed during the Famine, are false.
4. The Famine was not, as is often alleged, related to drought.
5. In 1931–32, the official Soviet response to a drought-induced grain shortage outside Ukraine was to send aid to the areas affected and to make a series of concessions to the peasantry.
6. In mid-1932, following complaints by officials in the Ukrainian SSR that excessive grain procurements had led to localized outbreaks of famine, Moscow reversed course and took an increasingly hard line toward the peasantry.
7. The inability of Soviet authorities in Ukraine to meet the grain procurements quota forced them to introduce increasingly severe measures to extract the maximum quantity of grain from the peasants.
8. In the Fall of 1932 Stalin used the resulting "procurements crisis" in Ukraine as an excuse to tighten his control in Ukraine and to intensify grain seizures further.
9. The Ukrainian Famine of 1932–1933 was caused by the maximum extraction of agricultural produce from the rural population.

---

[10] The changes in terminology are interesting. Conquest used "Terror-Famine"; the term "Ukrainian Holocaust" was popular among historians of Ukraine in North America in the 1980s and 1990s. But, as Kul'chyts'kyi (*Ukrains'kyi Holodomor v konteksti,* 168) has argued, it is a misleading and inappropriate term that blurs the lines between two altogether distinct events.

[11] The last three points of the Executive Summary, which relate to U.S. foreign policy and Western scholarship, have been omitted here.

10. Officials in charge of grain seizures also lived in fear of punishment.
11. Stalin knew that people were starving to death in Ukraine by late 1932.
12. In January 1933, Stalin used the "laxity" of the Ukrainian authorities in seizing grain to strengthen further his control over the Communist Party of Ukraine and mandated actions that worsened the situation and maximized the loss of life.
13. Postyshev had a dual mandate from Moscow: to intensify the grain seizures (and therefore the Famine) in Ukraine and to eliminate such modest national self-assertion as Ukrainians had hitherto been allowed by the USSR.
14. While famine also took place during the 1932–1933 agricultural year in the Volga Basin and the North Caucasus Territory as a whole, the invasiveness of Stalin's interventions in both the Fall of 1932 and January 1933 in Ukraine are paralleled only in the ethnically Ukrainian Kuban region of the North Caucasus.
15. Attempts were made to prevent the starving from travelling to areas where food was more available.
16. Joseph Stalin and those around him committed genocide against Ukrainians in 1932–1933.

In many ways, Mace set the agenda for research on the Holodomor. The questions he raised regarding intentions, policy, and practice were subsequently taken up by an entire generation of historians of Ukraine. Stanislav Kul'chyts'kyi ("Dzheims Meis") has written movingly about his encounters—sometimes contentious—with Mace and the influence that Mace exercised on his own work and thinking in the early 1990s (See also Vasyl'iev, "Evoliutsiia"). This does not, in any way, diminish the tremendous amount of research that has been done by Kul'chyts'kyi and many other researchers over the last two decades. On the contrary, it is owing to them that Mace's findings remain relevant today.[12] We now have a much more substantial and more refined picture of what happened across Ukraine in 1932–1933.

---

[12] In the Report to Congress (xv), Mace, for example, concluded that Stalin knew that people were starving to death on the basis of a 1964 account published in *Pravda* by Roman Terekhov, who served as a member of the CP(b)U Politburo and Kharkiv regional secretary until late January 1933. Terekhov wrote that he personally told Stalin in December 1932 about the desperate situation in the villages of the Kharkiv region. Historians have now found many documents confirming Stalin's awareness of the Famine.

What have we learned? Here are some of the key discoveries and developments in recent years, using Mace's original findings as a reference. The list is by no means exhaustive.

1. Demographic losses. How many people died as a result of the Holodomor in Ukraine?

In 1988, in his Report to Congress, Mace was careful not to name an exact number, arguing that the available information was still too unreliable. He guessed at the time that the range was somewhere between 3 and 8 million. In the last decade, several teams of demographers, using increasingly sophisticated and complex methods, have attempted to estimate the losses incurred during the Holodomor. Historians and demographers are now beginning to settle on a range of 2.5 to 4 million excess deaths. In 2002 an international team led by the French demographer Jacques Vallin estimated losses at between 2.6 to 3.6 million people (Vallin et al., 262). In 2008, the Institute for Demography and Social Studies of the National Academy of Sciences of Ukraine projected a range of 3.4–3.9 million excess deaths during the years 1932–34 (Wolowyna, "The Famine-Genocide" 63; Libanova 29). As virtually every demographer and historian who has considered this question has noted, however, a precise figure cannot be established because of serious problems with Soviet census materials, especially the 1937 and 1939 data. The breakdown of recordkeeping in 1933, at the height of the Famine, further complicates the issue (Wolowyna, "Holodomor Losses"; Shevchuk; Rudnyts'kyi and Savchuk).

It should be noted, moreover, that the number of excess deaths cited above does not capture the full extent of the demographic catastrophe—the drop in the birth rate, the fall in life expectancy, and the demographic trough created by the deaths of so many infants and children, for example. According to Kyiv demographers, lost births alone account for perhaps an additional one million (Wolowyna "Famine-Genocide" 62; Libanova "Otsinka" 276).[13]

Some of the most interesting research currently underway concerns regional variations in demographic losses (Levchuk, Wheatcroft,

---

[13] In 2009, the SBU (Security Service of Ukraine) estimated that Ukraine suffered a population loss of 10 million people—3.9 million excess deaths and 6.1 million in lost births (Sukhomlin). The latter figure assumes that the exceptionally high fertility rate of the 1920s could have lasted until the 1930s. This assumption is rejected by Vallin, Wolowyna and others.

Rudnyts'kyi et al.).[14] (The *National Book of Memory* project served as an important stimulus in this regard.) Preliminary results suggest that population losses were highest in Kyiv and Kharkiv oblasts, and lowest—excluding the Moldavian Autonomous Republic —in Donetsk and Chernihiv (Levchuk 261). (Ukraine in 1932–33 consisted of seven oblasts: Vynnytsia, Dnipropetrovsk, Donetsk, Kyiv, Odesa, Kharkiv, Chernihiv and the Moldavian Autonomous Republic.) Without more research on migration patterns, resettlement policies and local history in the late 1920s and early 1930s, however, it is far too early to arrive at any definitive conclusions about the meaning of these regional differences.

2. Methods. How was the Holodomor implemented?

We have learned much more about the specific measures and practices that were introduced in Ukraine and the Kuban in 1932–33, the mechanisms by which people were starved to death. As the economic historian Michael Ellman put it so clearly (Ellman 680), the Holodomor was not simply an act of omission—failing to request or accept offers of relief from abroad. It was an act of commission. From impossibly high grain procurement quotas, to the decree of 20 November 1932 that halted the payment of grain to collective farm workers until their grain delivery quotas had been met, to the forcible removal of food from houses, there were special punitive measures that were introduced.

In particular, there has been substantial research on the practice of blacklisting villages, the so-called *chorni doshky*—a practice that was used widely in Ukraine and the Kuban in 1932–33. Heorhii Papakin, senior researcher at the Institute of History, Academy of Sciences of Ukraine, has been studying the subject for over a decade and has compiled a 180 page-long list of villages and collective farms in Ukraine that were blacklisted ("'Chorni doshky' iak oblychchia"). On the basis of his extensive work, it is fair to say that the practice of blacklisting villages was much more extensive and discriminatory than had previously been known (Papakin).

For a village to be blacklisted meant that 1) all stores would be closed and supplies removed from the village; 2) all trade was prohibited, including trade in food or grain; 3) all loans and advances were called in, including grain advances; 4) the local Party and collective farm organizations were purged, and usually subject to arrest; 5) food and

---

[14]The Harvard Ukrainian Research Institute has also launched a Geographic Information System (GIS) project aimed at creating a digital atlas of the Holodomor in Ukraine. See <http://gis.huri.harvard.edu/>

livestock would be confiscated as a "penalty"; and 6) the territory would be sealed off by OGPU (secret police) detachments. In other words, residents had their supplies of food taken away and they were not allowed to leave. In effect, as Kul'chyts'kyi and others have argued, it was a death sentence imposed on the population (Kul'chyts'kyi "Holodomor 1932–33 rr.: Mekhanizm" 8; Papakin "Neopublikovani" 46).

The system of blacklisting was formalized by a Decree of 20 November 1932 titled, "The Struggle against Kurkul Influence in Collective Farms" [*Pro borot'bu z kurkul's'kym vplyvom v kolhospakh*]. As Papakin has pointed out, however, the target of the blacklists were often not collective farms that had fallen behind in their grain deliveries or private farmers who failed to pay their tax in kind, but rather entire villages. That is, *all* of the inhabitants of a village were branded as kurkuls/kulaks and punished—even those who were not directly involved in the production of grain (blacksmiths, teachers, children, etc.) ("Neopublikovani" 46-47). The quota was only one criterion; there were very few collective farms that were able to meet their assigned quotas anywhere in Ukraine in the winter of 1932–33. The size of the village as well as its prominence in the region factored in the decision (from the internal correspondence it is clear that the practice of blacklisting villages was intended to serve as a warning for the surrounding population).[15] The political past of the village, however, was also an important determinant. Villages with known supporters of the Ukrainian People's Republic in 1919 and/or with a history of resistance to Bolshevik grain requisitioning during the civil war and collectivization were singled out. The entire village of Mazurivka in Vinnytsia oblast, for example, was blacklisted because it was the birthplace of one of Petliura's military commanders, Otaman Khmara (Papakin "'Chorni doshky' iak oblychchia" 4-6). On the basis of his extensive research, Papakin has concluded that the practice of blacklisting had a political as well as ethno-social dimension. For example, Cossack villages were a special target in the Volga region and, of course, in the Kuban. It was, in his words, a form of political retribution against those groups who had, in the past, demonstrated their opposition to the Soviet regime (Papakin *'Chorna doshka': Antyselians'ki* 338).

According to Papakin, there were blacklisted villages in all of the oblasts of Ukraine, and in some districts/raions, virtually every settlement was included. In Vinnytsia, there were five entire raions that were

---

[15] According to Papakin, settlements were chosen by local raion Party committees that were under great pressure from "above," from Kosior and Chubar and especially Kaganovich. Kaganovich also supported the idea of economic blockades of the raions that were farthest behind in delivering grain.

blacklisted; in Dnipropetrovsk, every single raion had blacklisted villages (Papakin "'Chorni doshky' v Ukraini: mekhanizm" 6-7, 13). Papakin believes, on the basis of preliminary research, that there is a strong correlation between blacklisting and mortality—but, as he himself admits, this requires further study (Papakin "'Chorni doshky' iak oblychchia" 7).[16]

The other major revelation was the discovery of the existence of a formal decree prohibiting peasants in Ukraine and the Kuban from leaving starvation-hit areas in search of food in neighbouring regions of the Soviet Union. The secret directive issued in Moscow on 22 January 1933 was simply entitled, "Preventing the Mass Exodus of Peasants Who Are Starving" (*Dyrektyva TsK VKP(b) i RNK SRSR "Pro zapobihannia masovoho vyizdu selian, iaki holoduiut'" vid 22 sichnia 1933 r.*). It prohibited the sale of tickets for transport by train or boat to peasants. In effect, the borders of Soviet Ukraine and the Kuban were closed by the secret police and militia detachments. In the six weeks after the decree was issued, nearly 220,000 people were arrested, an astonishingly high number (Danilov 3: 634-35; Pyrih 609-16; Ivnitskii 204).

Mace had concluded on the basis of anecdotal evidence that this was, in fact, the policy. Now, as we know, it was a formal order signed by Stalin himself. This is what the historian Roman Serbyn has called the "smoking gun." The directive, he concluded is "perhaps the best available proof of the dictator's genocidal intent against the Ukrainian nation" (Serbyn "Smoking Gun").

Finally, new studies have revealed the very selective—indeed, highly politicized—nature of state assistance in Ukraine in 1932-33. Soviet authorities, as we know, took great pains to guarantee the supply of food to the industrial workforce and to certain other categories of the population—Red Army personnel and their families, for example. As the latest research has shown, however, in the spring of 1933, famine relief itself became an ideological instrument. The aid that was provided in rural Ukraine at the height of the Famine, when much of the population was starving, was directed, first and foremost, to "conscientious" collective farm workers—those who had worked the highest number of workdays. Rations, as the sources attest, were allocated in connection with spring sowing (T. Boriak 18-21; Werth).[17] The bulk of assistance was delivered in the form of grain

---

[16] Stephen Wheatcroft (219-25) recently challenged the notion that there was a correlation between blacklisting villages and mortality based on raion (district) data. Without reliable data and local history *at the village level*, however, it is premature to dismiss the significance or outcomes of "blacklisting."

[17] This stands in sharp contrast to 1932, when famine relief was distributed,

seed that was "lent" to collective farms (from reserves that had been seized in Ukraine) with the stipulation that it would be repaid with interest (T. Boriak 15–16). State aid, it seems clear, was aimed at trying to salvage the collective farm system and a workforce necessary to maintain it. At the very same time, Party officials announced a campaign to root out "enemy elements of all kinds who sought to exploit the food problems for their own counter-revolutionary purposes, spreading rumours about the famine and various 'horrors'" (Werth, fn 25: Vasyl'iev, "Porivnial'nyi analiz" 127). Famine relief, in this way, became yet another way to determine who lived and who died.

3. Stalin. What have we learned about Stalin and his intentions?

The question of intentions has always been at heart of the discussion of the Holodomor. In his report to Congress, James Mace concluded—again, on the basis of anecdotal evidence—that "Stalin knew that people were starving to death in Ukraine by late 1932." Historians of Ukraine have been keenly interested in this problem for a very long time: What did the Kremlin know, when did they know it, and how did they respond to the information they had? A number of scholars, including Stanislav Kul'chyts'kyi, Mykola Doroshko, Iurii Shapoval, and Valerii Vasyl'iev, have written extensively on relations between the Kremlin and the leadership of the Ukrainian Communist Party.[18] The relationship between Kharkiv and local Party organizations has also been a subject of interest. In part, this is a response to suggestions by some historians that the particular viciousness and lethalness of the Famine-Terror in Ukraine may have been a reflection of the way that local leaders interpreted policy rather than the policies and measures themselves (Vasyl'iev, "Osoblyvosti" 1). The publication in 2008 of *Holodomor 1932–33 rokiv v Ukraini: dokumenty i materialy*—a 1,125-page collection of Russian and Ukrainian archival documents relating to the Holodomor under the auspices of the Institute of History of the Academy of Sciences of Ukraine—has, in addition, greatly advanced our understanding in these areas (Pyrih).

This research put to rest, once and for all, any notion that Stalin and his circle might have been unaware of how grave the situation in Ukraine was in 1932 and 1933. Ukraine was in crisis by the winter of 1931–32, as numerous letters and documents attest. There was evidence of famine,

---

generally, in famine-stricken areas through canteens.

[18] Cf. Vasyl'ev, "Osoblyvosti"; Vasyl'ev and Shapoval; Doroshko; Kul'chyts'kyi, *Ukrains'kyi Holodomor v konteksti,* and his "Stalins'ka dyktatura."

people were starving to death, there were reports of cannibalism, some were beginning to flee the village, popular opposition was growing, farmers were slaughtering livestock, armed grain collection brigades were roaming the countryside, violence was mounting, the agricultural sector appeared to be collapsing, there was unrest in the Party, and, in some areas, Soviet authority itself was breaking down. There was genuine concern in Kharkiv as to whether the peasants would even have the capacity to undertake another growing season. Several Ukrainian Communist Party leaders, most notably Vlas Chubar, the Chairman of the Ukrainian Council of People's Commissars (*Radnarkom*; Russ: *Sovnarkom*), and Hryhorii Petrovs'kyi, Chairman of the Central Executive Committee of the Soviet Union, made repeated efforts, beginning in March 1932, to alert Stalin and the Politburo and to seek some form of relief—even as they continued to execute their orders (Kul'chyts'kyi, *Ukrains'kyi Holodomor v konteksti*, ch. 5). The letters that Chubar and Petrovs'kyi wrote to the Kremlin on 10 June—cited widely by scholars—are merely part of an ongoing exchange between Kharkiv and Moscow about the situation in Ukraine (Davies et al. 167-70, 180-81). Stalin, as we now know, was very much a "hands-on" leader, intimately involved in the details of administration. He himself expressed concern on numerous occasions, most notably in a letter to Lazar Kaganovich on 11 August 1932: "At this point the question of Ukraine is the most important. The situation in Ukraine is terrible. If we don't take steps now to improve the situation, we may lose Ukraine" (Davies et al. 180).

Stalin responded to the crisis in a manner that we now know was typical—he blamed the "Ukrainians" (his words), Chubar and Kosior, and others—for the failures. And his solution, ultimately, was to intensify the use of force and repression. "The Soviet leadership understood that catastrophe was looming," Valerii Vasyl'iev wrote in his study of the Soviet leadership. "Molotov, upon returning from Ukraine [in the summer of 1932], admitted at a meeting of the Politburo that 'We are on the verge of famine in many of the grain-growing districts.'" The Politburo, however, decided to "go ahead with the grain procurement plan at all costs" (Vasyl'iev, "Osoblyvosti" 5; Ivnitskii *Golod* 355).

What this research has revealed, quite clearly, is the "Ukrainian vector" of the Famine—the political dimension of Stalin's thinking and the special fixation he had on Ukraine. It was, in his own words, "a distinctive republic." "The most important issue right now is Ukraine," he emphasized in his correspondence. By Stalin's own admission, the campaign of 1932-33 in Ukraine was not just about grain. It was part of a larger political battle for Ukraine, a fight against what he deemed "counter-revolution" (Davies et al. 180-81). Stalin himself, we now know, was under threat from critics within the Party. The battle for Ukraine thus became, as Stanislav Kul'chyts'kyi has argued, part of Stalin's own struggle against those who blamed him for the disasters of collectivization (Kul'chyts'kyi *Ukrains'kyi Holodomor v konteksti* 102–103). Ukrainian Communists, in particular, were not to be trusted. The Party, Stalin believed, was full of "rotten elements, conscious and instinctive adherents of Petliura, and direct agents of Piłsudski." For Stalin, as Lars Lih, one of the editors of the Stalin-Molotov correspondence, has observed, governing was an "eternal battle" with "saboteurs" (Lih et al. 17). In the early fall of 1932, the Kremlin prepared for a decisive battle, mobilizing the Party, military, and the secret service for the campaign. Each grain collection brigade was to be escorted by military units as well as shock brigades of militant Communists. It was, in effect, a counter-insurgency launched against an unarmed civilian population. As Ukraine began once again to fall behind in its grain deliveries, Stalin sent his most trusted lieutenants, first Molotov then Postyshev, to oversee the operation, to purge the Party of unreliable elements, and, ultimately, to deliver the "shattering blow" (*sokrushitel'nyi udar*), as Stalin put it. The "shattering blow," Kul'chyts'kyi has argued, was the instruction on 18 November 1932, to conduct house-to-house searches for "stolen grain" and to permit the confiscation of all food, including meat and potatoes, as a penalty (Kul'chyts'kyi, *Ukrains'kyi Holodomor v konteksti* 102–103).[19]

What is now also clear is the direct connection in Stalin's mind between the difficulties of grain procurement and the policy of Ukrainization. This is something that historians who do not study Ukraine often ignore. The incorrect policy of Ukrainization, Stalin claimed, had given legal cover to all manner of "bourgeois nationalists," "Petliurites" and kulaks (Ukrainian: *kurkuls*) who were based in the countryside, and who had "infiltrated" the collective farms as "administrators, accountants, warehouse supervisors, millers, members of village soviets, and cooperatives." They were now actively working to organize a counter-revolution and to sabotage the collection of grain. On 14 December 1932, he signed a decree ordering the arrests of these counter-revolutionaries, the expulsion of the "Petliurites and other bourgeois nationalist elements" from the Party and all Soviet institutions, and the closing down of all Ukrainian newspapers and journals.

---

[19] Stalin used the term "shattering blow" at a meeting of the Politburo and Presidium of the Central Committee of the Party on 27 November 1932 while defending himself against allegations that he was responsible for the failure of the grain procurement campaign. He blamed the failures on anti-Soviet elements ("Petliurites") who had infiltrated the collective farms and local Communist Party officials. The only correct response, he argued, was to deliver the "shattering blow."

In the Kuban, it brought an end to Ukrainian language education as well (Pyrih 475–77).

The struggle against "counter-revolutionary" elements thus served as a pretext for a massive purge of the Communist Party of Ukraine and collective farm administrations (fifty percent of collective farm chairs and their assistants), as well as the arrest of tens of thousands of people. (Some 125,000 people were arrested in 1933.) Thousands were sent to concentration camps. Hundreds of Ukrainian intellectuals were expelled from their research institutions, especially those associated in some way with Mykola Skrypnyk, the Commissar of Education in Ukraine and a leading proponent of Ukrainization. Entire institutions like the Bahalii Research Institute of History and Culture and the Ukrainian Soviet Encyclopedia were eventually closed down. Pavel Postyshev would later declare that 1933 was "the year of the defeat of Ukrainian nationalist counter-revolution" (Postyshev 165).[20]

4. Was it genocide?

The emergence of Genocide Studies as a distinct academic field since the late 1990s has exerted a powerful influence on the study of the Holodomor. In particular, the rediscovery, or rather discovery, of Rafael Lemkin, the originator of the concept of genocide, the spirit behind the U.N. Convention on the Prevention and Punishment of the Crime of Genocide, and the pioneer of Genocide Studies, has excited many scholars of the Holodomor (Antonovych; Serbyn, "Ukrainian Famine"; Klid and Motyl). Lemkin's notion of genocide, which he began to develop in the interwar period, was intrinsically linked to colonialism and the practices of settlement and occupation. It is precisely this broad approach that has proven so attractive to historians of Ukraine—Lemkin's view of genocide as a complex process with *many* forms, including political, economic, and cultural coercion, and not just physical violence. Genocide, in this respect, did "not necessarily mean immediate destruction" but, rather, targeting the institutions, culture and the economic existence of a group (Lemkin *Axis Rule* 79).

Ukraine, as researchers have discovered, was crucial to Lemkin's thinking about genocide. This he made clear in a previously unpublished essay written in 1953, i.e., on the twentieth anniversary of the Holodomor. It was intended as a chapter of a larger book entitled *History of Genocide*. In

---

[20] On the arrests and the campaign against Ukrainization, see Vasyl'ev, "Osoblyvosti"; Danylenko and Bondarchuk; Kocherha; Iefimenko.

this essay, Lemkin argued that Ukraine was a "classical example of Soviet genocide, its longest and broadest experiment in Russification—the destruction of the Ukrainian nation" (Lemkin, "Soviet Genocide" 235-42). The Holodomor (he, of course, did not use this word) was merely one episode of this extended process. The repeated attacks on Ukrainian intellectuals, the assault on religion and the Ukrainian churches, the dispersal and fragmentation of the Ukrainian people—all of these were part of a larger pattern. "The genocide was not that Stalin's regime killed so many people," as one Lemkin scholar explained, "but that these individuals were killed with the purpose of destroying the Ukrainian way of life" (Irvin-Erickson 68).

For historians of Ukraine, the emergence of Genocide Studies and the rediscovery of Rafael Lemkin have helped to reframe the problem of "intentions" and have greatly expanded the discussion of what constitutes genocide.[21] Like Lemkin, many scholars have come to view the Holodomor as merely one episode in a much longer and more complex history of coercion, suppression, and violence aimed at the destruction of Ukrainians as a people, a history they believe began well before 1932-33 and continued well beyond it.[22] In this respect, the link between colonialism and genocide—a link emphasized by genocide scholars like A. Dirk Moses and promoted most recently by the historian Mark von Hagen—has opened up new ways to conceptualize the genocidal nature of the Holodomor (von Hagen; McDonnell and Moses).

Other historians of Ukraine, in making the argument for genocide, continue to accentuate the uniquely lethal and punitive aspects of the Holodomor.[23] The numbers in themselves, they stress, are astounding, unprecedented in European history, much less the history of Ukraine. Ukraine lost a substantial part of its population *in a matter of a few months* in 1933 (February-July) (Volovyna). It was not, moreover, simply a matter of "bungling" or "indifference." These staggering losses were the result of decisions taken in the winter of 1932-33, decisions that "willfully"

---

[21] Among legal scholars, there has been a vigorous discussion and reappraisal of "intent" as it applies to the definition of genocide, especially since the creation of the International Criminal Court. Cf. Ambos, Greenawalt.

[22] The notion of three "Holodomors" (1921-1923, 1932-1933, 1946-1947) is one expression of this interpretation. Cf. Antonovych; Veselova "Holod"; Veselova and Marochko; and Odynoka.

[23] Cf. Kul'chyts'kyi, Shapoval, Vasyl'iev, Verstiuk, Graziosi, Vasylenko, Werth. Of course, the two approaches to understanding the Holodomor as genocide are not mutually exclusive.

maximized the losses in Ukraine and in the Kuban. Here, as Andrea Graziosi notes, the "scale of both punishment and terror reached extreme dimensions... thus growing into a qualitatively different phenomenon" ("Soviet Famines" 108). During the Holodomor, as millions of people were dying, the authorities waged a war against "Ukrainian nationalism." The attack on the Ukrainian countryside, in conjunction with the large-scale assault on the Ukrainian church, and Ukrainian rural and urban elites, were an attempt to crush Ukrainians, these historians argue, and thus constitute an act of genocide by the terms of the U.N. Convention.

5. Contested History

Of course, not all historians of Ukraine have been persuaded by the genocide argument. Most notably, Valerii Soldatenko, the former Director of the Institute of National Memory, rejected the application of the concept of genocide to events in Ukraine in 1932–33, while at the same time deploring the "politicization" of the issue (Soldatenko, "Trahediia" 4–8).[24] For him, as for other like-minded historians, the problem turns on the issue of intentions: "There is not a single document that supports the concept of the Holodomor as genocide in Ukraine or that even hints at ethnic motives" ("Trahediia" 20).

What happened in Ukraine in 1932–33 must be understood in a larger geopolitical context—the threat of war and the urgent need to industrialize in preparation for it. The aim of collectivization, first and foremost, according to this view, was the mobilization of resources for industrialization and the reorganization and modernization of the agricultural economy. Overcoming the resistance of the peasantry, however, was a necessary part of this process. As Soldatenko acknowledges, "these policies resulted in the massive disorganization of the agrarian sector of the economy and they were carried out, in some cases, with extreme violence against the peasant population. (He recognizes that the economic policies were a failure in the short term.) The famine was not a uniquely Ukrainian experience but rather a "common tragedy shared by all the people of the former Soviet Union," Soldatenko has concluded, echoing the argument made by Russian historians. As evidence of this, he cites the higher death rates in the North Caucasus, Kazakhstan, and in the Volga German Republic ("Trahediia" 22; "Prychyny").

---

[24] Soldatenko treated H. Kas'ianov, V. Kharchenko, and D. Viedienieiev as historians of Ukraine.

What is significant here—and a measure of how much the understanding of the Holodomor has changed—is the very narrowness of the debate that Soldatenko describes. Even the opponents of the concept of the Holodomor as genocide accept the basic outlines of what happened. Among historians, there is no significant argument over the number of people who died. There is a general agreement that they died as a result of the policies implemented by the Party leadership, the introduction of unrealistically high grain quotas, and the confiscation of grain resources and food. Historians of Ukraine are no longer debating whether the Famine was the result of natural causes. The academic debate appears to come down to the issue of intentions, to whether the special measures undertaken in Ukraine in the winter of 1932–33 that intensified starvation were aimed at Ukrainians as such. For Soldatenko, however, the debate is really about the *significance* of what happened—no small issue, by any means. For him and others, the Holodomor was the tragic price—a terribly steep but ultimately justifiable price—that was paid for "modernization."

6. Decentring History

Curiously, what has largely been missing from the academic literature until recently are Ukrainians themselves—the millions of ordinary men and women who experienced de-kulakization, collectivization, and the Holodomor. That may seem like a preposterous statement in light of the enormous efforts that have been made to collect and publish eyewitness testimonies, to identify and inscribe the names of people who died during the Holodomor, and to create a "national memory." Many oral history projects have been undertaken in the last twenty years, most notably, of course, *The National Book of Memory* (*Natsional'na Knyha pam'iati*) project in which thousands of local historians, archival workers, teachers and students participated.

Yet we still know relatively little about the lives of these people beyond the names. Among historians of Ukraine, much of the focus of research has been on "seeing like a state," to use the James C. Scott's celebrated phrase.[25] Much of the work has emphasized the intentions, policy, and methods of the Soviet leadership, much of the story has been about Stalin and Molotov, Kaganovich and Kosior and Chubar—and what they thought, how they spoke, and what they did.[26] One of the consequences—no doubt

---

[25] Though he does not discuss the Terror-Famine, Scott does write about Soviet collectivization as a notable example of high modernist ideology (see Scott).
[26] The need to understand the intentions of the Soviet authorities was also keenly

unintended—of the genocide debate that has dominated scholarship for nearly twenty years is that it tended to marginalize the people who experienced the Holodomor, rendering them into ghosts who silently haunt our work.[27] Their accounts as yet remain distant from the academic literature, summoned—if summoned at all—mainly as witnesses to the terrible deeds committed by "others." What we lack, for the most part, is a rich, full-blooded, detailed "history from below."

This observation is not intended to disparage the efforts of those scholars who work on Soviet policy and intentions. Nor is it meant to discount the work of all of those many, many individuals who have collected oral histories of the Holodomor. This kind of research is vitally necessary and important—in ways that go well beyond scholarship. Indeed, one of the hidden casualties of the Holodomor was social memory itself. After 1932–33, the Ukrainian village lost much of its autonomous capacity to tell stories, to relate its own collective history, to construct its own portrait of itself. In this respect, oral history is a way of restoring that capacity, of rebuilding collective memory and identity, perhaps even a way of healing what James Mace called a "post-genocidal society." The very act of consulting elderly rural residents—often women, the most impoverished and neglected segment of the population—is in itself a powerfully transformative exercise.

There is a crucial difference, however, between collecting oral history and critically analyzing testimonies, between gathering evidence and relating that evidence to larger social and cultural patterns, between publishing eyewitness accounts and writing social history. And when it comes to the Holodomor, there is still a very long way to go. Social history remains, without doubt, a largely unexplored frontier.[28]

Perhaps the first real glimpse into the momentous possibilities of a decentred history—and of the very significance of this approach—was the research done in the 1990s by Andrea Graziosi (*The Great Soviet Peasant War*), Lynne Viola (*Peasant Rebels under Stalin Collectivization and the Culture of Peasant Resistance*), and Liudmyla Hrynevych ("Stalins'ka

---

felt among survivors. In his memoirs, Miron Dolot, a Famine survivor and author of a rare full-length personal account of the Holodomor, could not resist interpreting the motives and intentions of the authorities (see Dolot).

[27] Increasingly, because they provide a glimpse of local practice, eyewitness accounts have become important in corroborating, expanding on and, in some cases, contradicting official documents (see Veselova, "Svidchennia ochevydtsiv").

[28] Liudmyla Hrynevych's magnum opus, *Khronika kolektyvizatsii ta Holodomoru v Ukraini 1927–1933*, is the most ambitious attempt to fill this gap. As of this writing, the first volume of four has been published.

'Revoliutsiia zhory'") on resistance to state policies in Ukraine between 1928 and 1933.[29] Ukraine, during collectivization, as Lynne Viola noted in her book, "led [the Soviet Union] in revolt." The revolts in Ukraine tended to be frequent, large, and occasionally violent, especially during periods of grain requisitioning. In 1930, at the height of resistance, according to OGPU sources, the participants numbered close to a million. "Throughout Ukraine," as Viola describes, "peasants rose up in defense of their property, neighbours, and culture, displaying a sense of political and national outrage and purpose unparalleled in the [Soviet Union]" (Viola 158–59). Liudmyla Hrynevych's work picks up where Viola's left off, and provides a fuller picture of the nature of these protests, the degree to which they became more organized and overtly anti-Soviet and anti-colonial during this period.

The real breakthrough of this work was in the approach, in the foregrounding of previously marginalized actors. They were histories of ordinary people, how they thought, how they behaved, and how they attempted to survive under extraordinary circumstances. It was a history that exposed the uneven character of Soviet power. Collectivization, as Viola explained, was not just an economic policy, it was a "clash of cultures," "a wholesale assault on the cultural traditions and institutions of the village," most notably the church. This is how the peasants understood it, as "a battle over their culture and way of life, as pillage, injustice and wrong." It was a "struggle for power and control," an attempt to subjugate them (Viola 14). And the Holodomor, if we take Viola's argument to its logical conclusion, was the climax of this life-and-death struggle.

This theme—the Holodomor era as a "cultural war"—has begun to receive greater attention among scholars of Ukraine in recent years and represents a crucial trend in the scholarship. In particular, it is ethnographers in Ukraine who have led the way in attempting to assess the cultural impact of collectivization, de-kulakization, and the Terror-Famine. It is ethnographers who have also—not surprisingly—made the greatest use of eyewitness accounts. William Noll, an American ethnomusicologist, and his team of Ukrainian researchers, did the pioneering work in this field. Between 1993 and 1995, they conducted interviews with 450 elderly rural residents in eastern and southern Ukraine in an attempt to understand how village life changed in the 1920s and 1930s. As described in their book—*Transformatsiia hromadians'koho suspil'stva. Usna istoriia selians'koi kul'tury 1920–30 rokiv* [*The Transformation of Civil Society: An Oral History*

---

[29] Though not as well known, the early research by Valerii Vasil'ev cited by Viola in her own book should be added to this list.

of Peasant Culture in the 1920s and 1930s]—the Holodomor era not only resulted in the deaths of millions of people. It radically changed the Ukrainian village; it led to the material impoverishment of the peasantry. It did away with entire categories of craftsmen, village residents and artists (icon painters, fiddlers, and other itinerant musical performers like the blind *startsi*). And, ultimately, it led to the decline, indeed destruction, of many traditional practices and institutions. Cultural practices associated with the church and religious holidays were special targets—not just baptisms, church weddings, and church funerals, which were central events in the life of country folk, but also *koliadky* (Christmas carols) and *vesnianky* (spring songs).

Indeed, as Noll and his colleagues discovered, the very tenor of everyday life was transformed during the Holodomor era. Even the seemingly innocent traditional practices like the *dosvitky*—the ritual gatherings of young unmarried women who met every evening in the winter to sew and embroider and sing—were suppressed. Village clubs, organized and managed by Party officials, replaced them. In the final analysis, Noll argued, collectivization, de-kulakization, and the Terror-Famine were a "cultural catastrophe."

More recently, Olesia Stasiuk published a bold new study of the Ukrainian village during the Holodomor era entitled *Henotsyd ukraintsiv: deformatsiia narodnoi kul'tury* (*Genocide of Ukrainians: The Deformation of National Culture*). In contrast to Noll, Stasiuk was interested in the larger social consequences of collectivization and the Terror-Famine, in the ways in which individuals and families were affected. In often harrowing terms, she describes the violence with which the policy of collectivization and grain requisitioning was often implemented—how ordinary people were humiliated, ostracized, and terrorized. She discusses the mass flight from the countryside and the breakdown and destruction of the family. But Stasiuk was also interested in the effects of the Holodomor on social mores: the rise of the culture of denunciations (*donosy*), the increase in petty theft. *Henotsyd ukraintsiv*, perhaps more than any other academic work to date, illustrates what it meant *to live through* the Holodomor.

Regional and local histories represent another promising trend in Ukrainian historiography. A number of studies have been produced in recent years focusing on the Holodomor at the oblast and even village level.[30] (The *National Book of Memory* series, with seventeen separate

---

[30] See Iatsenko; Starovoitov and Mykhailychenko; Akunin; Matvieiev; Pshenychnyi; Bakhtin.

regional volumes, provided an important stimulus to research in this area.) The value of this approach, it goes without saying, is in illuminating how policy and directives were put into practice and how, on the other hand, various groups and individuals, including local Party officials, responded to the severe challenges posed by the Holodomor. Ultimately, such histories will also help to shed light on regional variations, including differences in population losses already noted by demographers. At present, however, this area of research remains at a very early stage in its development, the results are quite uneven, and scholars are not yet in any position to offer a meaningful comparative analysis.

Indeed, there are many gaps in the historiography. There is still no systematic study of the strategies that people used to try to survive the Holodomor. Not much is known about the other victims of the Holodomor—those hundreds of thousands of people who were arrested and/or exiled in 1932–33. The actual history and fate of blacklisted villages remain unexplored. There is very little scholarship on gender—Oksana Kis's ground-breaking work on women constitutes a notable exception (see Kis). Little has been written on the urban experience.[31] And, of course, there is no serious study of the "perpetrators," i.e., those who carried out orders in the Ukrainian countryside and who, in some cases, themselves became victims.[32] In this respect, Holodomor Studies is still a very new field of research.

7. The Impact on Ukrainian History: A Final Thought

Finally, let us consider our last question—what impact has the study of the Holodomor had on our understanding of Ukrainian history? There is no single answer to this question. For many historians of Ukraine, the significance of the Holodomor is measured in terms of the number of lives lost, in the size and scale of the demographic catastrophe. For Soldatenko and like-minded colleagues, the Holodomor was a terrible but necessary price to be paid for industrialization and modernization. For others, the Holodomor represents the darkest chapter in a whole series of violent assaults on the Ukrainian people perpetrated by a totalitarian state. The discussion, in many ways, continues to revolve around the Soviet paradigm.

---

[31] The exceptions here are the work of Borysenko and Kuromiya.

[32] The recent publication of documents relating to local Party activists in Ukraine by Vasyl'iev et al. (*Partiino-radians'ke kerivnytstvo*) is an important step and should facilitate further scholarship on the subject.

As someone who comes to the subject from the nineteenth century—from the study of Ukraine *before* the Soviet Union—I would like to suggest a different way of thinking about this problem. Viewed in a larger context, the Holodomor era—and here I would include de-kulakization, collectivization and the Terror-Famine—represents a considerable rupture in the history of Ukraine. In terms of patterns of migration, family structure, religious practices, rituals of courtship and marriage, names and naming practices, in terms of status and ranking, in terms of attitudes towards power, authority, and political participation, in terms of social identity, this period constitutes a radical break. The Holodomor era fundamentally changed the way Ukrainians (and others) lived.

The Holodomor also marks the violent end of a particular social order: the end of a set of social structures, social institutions and social practices associated with Cossack history and culture in Ukraine. It was a social order that had endured, with significant changes, of course, since the seventeenth century and that had come to be seen as manifestly Ukrainian. Long after the end of the Hetmanate, the destruction of the Sich, the incorporation of the officer class into the Russian nobility, and the expansion of serfdom, there were still ordinary Cossacks and Cossack settlements throughout "Malorossiia."[33] In Poltava and in large parts of Chernihiv gubernia at the beginning of the twentieth century, they represented nearly fifty percent of the population (Bachyns'ka 24). Here, in rural Ukraine, Cossack status served, in effect, as the line between freedom and bondage. The Cossacks remained a distinct group with distinct property rights and a distinct legal status until the twentieth century—a group, moreover, who consciously cultivated Cossack history and identity as an expression of their social standing.[34] The Revolution of 1917, as we know, reanimated the Cossack movement, especially on the territory of the former Hetmanate, and, ultimately, put it on a collision course with Soviet authorities.

The Holodomor era was the final chapter in this confrontation. It deprived the population of their land, the very foundation of their social organization. It erased their social identity, transforming and reducing a diverse rural population into "kulaks" and "peasants." It extinguished the

---

[33] Here I am referring to the descendants of the "registered Cossacks." Until the 1860s, Ukrainian Cossacks from "Malorossia" served as a reserve guard to be called up in case of war. They were also instrumental in the colonization of southern Ukraine and the Kuban (Bachyns'ka; Petrenko).

[34] One of the signs of the persistence and influence of this Cossack culture are the so-called "Cossack crosses," stone memorials, found in parts of central Ukraine. They continued to be erected for centuries until the 1930s (Zymovets').

last remnants of village autonomy. It destroyed a substantial part of the material culture. It devastated one of the vital seedbeds of the Ukrainian national movement. It eliminated, once and for all, the social basis of a very formidable political opponent. And, of course, the Holodomor destroyed many, many lives.

In this respect, I would argue, the era of the Holodomor was exceptional and represents a turning point, as momentous as perhaps any in Ukrainian history. The human losses were staggering, the social and cultural, not to mention psychological, consequences of de-kulakization, collectivization, and the Terror-Famine were profound. The Holodomor should not, for this reason, be conflated with other famines in Ukraine or even other social catastrophes of the twentieth century.

***

It has taken decades for the Holodomor to gain recognition as a legitimate subject of research. As Holodomor Studies continues to grow, the range of themes, approaches, and theories will continue to expand. Historians will no doubt discover fresh meanings and different patterns that will link the study of the Holodomor across boundaries to other scholarly problems and fields in new and interesting ways. The "decentring" of history is already underway and undoubtedly represents the future for Holodomor Studies.

WORKS CITED

Akunin, O. S. *Pivdennoukrains'ke selianstvo v kintsi 20-kh - pershii polovyni 30-kh rokiv XX st.: sotsial'no-ekonomichne stanovyshche*. Dnipropetrovsk: Dnipropetrovs'kyi natsional'nyi universytet im. O. Honchara, 2009. Print.

Ambos, Kai. "What does 'Intent To Destroy' in Genocide Mean?" *International Review of the Red Cross* 91.876 (2009): 833–58. Print.

Andriewsky, Olga, and Natalie Pringle. "Social Science Meets Memory: The Harvard Project on the Soviet Social System as a Source on the *Holodomor*." *Holodomor 1932–1933 rokiv v Ukraini: istoriia i pam'iat'*. Kyiv. 21 Nov. 2013. Unpublished conference paper.

Antonovych, Myroslava. "Holodomor 1932–1933 rokiv v Ukraini v konteksti radians'koho henotsydu proty ukrains'koi natsii." *Holodomor 1932–1933 rokiv v Ukraini iak zlochyn henotsydu zhidno z mizhnarodnym pravom*. Ed. Volodomyr Vasylenko and Myroslava Antonovych. Kyiv: Kyievo-Mohylians'ka akademiia, 2012. 74–94. Print.

Bachyns'ka, Olena. "Malorosiis'ki kozaky" XIX st.: sotsio-demohrafichna kharakterystyka ta terytorial'ne rozselennia." *Istoryko-heohrafichni doslidzhennia v Ukraini* 12 (2012): 15–26. Print.

Bakhtin, Anatolii M. *Kolektyvizatsiia sil's'koho hospodarstva i holod na terytorii pivdnia Ukrainy (1929–1933 rr.)*. Kyiv: Kyievo-Mohylians'ka akademiia, 2006. Print.

Boriak, H. V., and H. V. Papakin. "Holodomor v Ukraini 1932–1933: Reiester arkhivnykh dokumentiv, opublikovanykh u 1990–2007 rr." *Natsional'na Knyha pam'iati zhertv Holodomoru 1932–1933 rr. v Ukraini*. Kyiv: Vyd-vo im. O. Telihy, 2008. 421–532. Print.

Boriak, Tetiana. "Prodovol'cha dopomoha Kremlia iak instrument Holodomoru v Ukraini." *Zlochyny totalitarnykh rezhymiv v Ukraini: Naukovyi ta osvitnii pohliad*. Kyiv: NIOD & Ukrains'kyi tsentr vyvchennia istorii Holokostu, 2012. 10–33. Print.

Boryk, Jennifer. "Memory Politics: The Use of the Holodomor as a Political and Nationalistic Tool in Ukraine." MA thesis. Central European University, 2011. Print.

Borysenko, Valentyna. "Holodomor 1932–1933 rokiv u misti Kyievi ta peredmisti." *Etnichna istoriia narodiv Evropy* 25 (2008): 5–14. Print.

Botushans'ka, O. F., ed. *Holodomor v Ukraini 1932–1933 rr.: bibliohrafichnyi pokazhchyk*. 2 vols. Odesa and Lviv: Odes'ka derzhavna naukova biblioteka imeni M. Hor'koho; Instytut istorii Ukrainy NAN Ukrainy; Fundatsiia ukrainoznavchykh studii Avstralii, Vyd-vo M. P. Kots', 2001. Print.

Carynnyk, Marco. "Blind Eye to Murder: Britain, the United States and the Ukrainian Famine of 1933." *Famine in Ukraine 1932–1933*. Ed. Roman Serbyn and Bohdan Krawchenko. Edmonton: Canadian Institute of Ukrainian Studies, 1986. 109–38. Print.

---. "Making the News Fit to Print: Walter Duranty, the New York Times and the Ukrainian Famine of 1933." *Famine in Ukraine 1932–1933*. Eds. Roman Serbyn and Bohdan Krawchenko. Edmonton: Canadian Institute of Ukrainian Studies, 1986. 67–95. Print.

"Communist Ukrainian Institute Head Denies Famine Was Deliberate." *Radio Free Europe/Radio Liberty*. 29 July 2010. Web. 24 Oct. 2014.

Conquest, Robert. *The Harvest of Sorrow: Soviet Collectivization and the Terror-Famine*. New York: Oxford University Press, 1986. Print.

Danilov, Viktor Petrovich, and Lynne Viola. *Tragediia sovetskoi derevni: kollektivizatsiia i raskulachivanie: dokumenty i materialy v 5 tomakh, 1927–1939*. 5 Vols. Moscow: Rossiiskaia polit. entsiklopediia, 2001. Print.

Danylenko, Viktor, and Petro Bondarchuk. "'Ukrainizatsiia' i holod 1932–1933 rokiv v Ukraini." *Problemy istorii Ukrainy: fakty, sudzhennia, poshuky* 18 (2008): 327–35. Print.

Davies, R.W., O. V. Khlevniuk, and E. A. Rees, eds. *The Stalin-Kaganovich Correspondence, 1931–36*. New Haven: Yale University Press, 2003. Print.

Dolot, Miron. *Execution by Hunger: The Hidden Holocaust*. 1st ed. New York: W.W. Norton, 1985. Print.

---. *Who Killed Them and Why?: In Remembrance of Those Killed in the Famine of 1932–1933 in Ukraine*. Cambridge, MA: Harvard University Ukrainian Studies Fund, 1984. Print.

Doroshko, Mykola. "Kerivna verstva USRR v umovakh Holodomoru 1932–1933 rr." *Problemy istorii Ukrainy: fakty, sudzhennia, poshuky* 18 (2008): 75–91. Print.

---. "Partiini chystky iak zasib likvidatsii opozytsii v KP(b)U v 20–30-ti roky XX st." *Henotsyd ukrains'koho narodu: istorychna pam"iat' ta polityko-pravova otsinka*. Kyiv: Vyd-vo M. P. Kots', 2003. 136–48. Print.

"Dvi tretyny meshkantsiv krainy vvazhaiut' Holodomor henotsydom ukrains'koho narodu—opytuvannia." *Korrespondent* 11 Nov. 2013. Web. 24 Oct. 2014.

Ellman, Michael. "Stalin and the Soviet Famine of 1932–33 Revisited." *Europe–Asia Studies* 59.4 (2007): 663–93. Print.

Foucault, Michel. *Security, Territory, Population: Lectures at the Collège De France, 1977–1978*. Ed. Michel Senellart, François Ewald and Alessandro Fontana. New York: Picador/Palgrave Macmillan, 2009. Print.

Graziosi, Andrea. *The Great Soviet Peasant War: Bolsheviks and Peasants, 1917–1933. Harvard Papers in Ukrainian Studies*. Cambridge, MA: Ukrainian Research Institute, Harvard University, 1996. Print.

Graziosi, Andrea. "The Soviet 1931–1933 Famines and the Ukrainian Holodomor: Is a New Interpretation Possible, and What Would Its Consequences Be?" *Harvard Ukrainian Studies* 27.1–4 (2004–2005): 97–115. Print.

Greenawalt, Alexander K. A. "Rethinking Genocidal Intent. The Case for a Knowledge-Based Interpretation." *Columbia Law Review* 99 (1999): 2259–94. Print.

Hanzha, Oksana I. *Ukrains'ke selianstvo v period stanovlennia totalitarnoho rezhemu (1917–1927 rr.)*. Kyiv: Instytut istorii Ukrainy, NAN Ukrainy, 2000. Print.

Harvard Ukrainian Research Institute. "MAPA. Digital Atlas of Ukraine." 2013. Web. 24 Oct. 2014. <http://gis.huri.harvard.edu/>

Himka, John-Paul. "Encumbered Memory: The Ukrainian Famine of 1932–33." *Kritika* 14.2 (2013): 411–36. Print.

---. "Problems with the Category of Genocide and With Classifying the Ukrainian Famine of 1932–33 as a Genocide." *Holodomor 1932–1933 rokiv v Ukraini: prychyny, demohrafichni naslidky, pravova otsinka*. Kyiv: Kyiv-Mohyla Academy, 2009. 413–20. Print.

Holodomor 1932–1933. Web. 24 Oct. 2014. <http://holodomor33.org.ua>

Holodomor: Ukrainian Genocide in the Early 1930s. Kyiv: Ukrainian Institute of National Memory, 2008. Print.

Hrynevych, Liudmyla. *Khronika kolektyvizatsii ta Holodomoru v Ukraini 1927–1933*. Vol. 1, Books 1–3. Kyiv: Krytyka, 2008–2012. Print.

---. "Stalins'ka 'revoliutsiia zhory' ta holod 1933 r. iak faktory polityzatsii ukrains'koi spil'noty." *Ukrains'kyi istorychnyi zhurnal* 5 (2003): 50–64. Print.

---. "Tsina stalins'koi 'revoliutsii zhory': ukrains'ke selianstvo v ochikuvanni na viinu." *Problemy istorii Ukrainy: fakty, sudzhennia, poshuky* 16.1 (2007): 287–306. Print.

Iefimenko, H. H. "Zmina vektoriv u natsional'nii politytsi Moskvy v holodomornyi 1933 r." *Ukrains'kyi istorychnyi zhurnal* 5 (2003): 25–50. Print.

---. "Zminy v natsional'nii politytsi TsK VKP(b) v Ukraini (1932–1938)." *Ukrains'kyi istorychnyi zhurnal* 2 (2000): 82–93. Print.

Irvin-Erickson, Douglas. "Genocide, the 'Family of Mind' and the Romantic Signature of Raphael Lemkin." *Journal of Genocide Research* 15.3 (2013): 273–96. Print.

Ivnitskii, N. A. *Golod 1932–1933 godov v SSSR*. Moscow: Sobraniie, 2009. Print.

---. *Kollektivizatsiia i raskulachivanie (nachala 30-kh godov)*. Moscow: Magistr, 1996. Print.

"Iz Instituta Natspam'iati uvolen 'zashchitnik genotsida'." *LB.ua*. 16 Sept. 2010. Web. 24 Oct. 2014.

Kas'ianov, Heorhii. *Danse macabre: Holod 1932–1933 rokiv u polityi, masovii svidomosti ta istoriohrafii (1980-ti - pochatok 2000-kh)*. Kyiv: Nash chas, 2010. Print.

---. "Holodomor and the Politics of Memory in Ukraine after Independence." *Holodomor and Gorta Mór: Histories, Memories and Representations of Famine in Ukraine and Ireland*. Ed. Lindsay Janssen, Vincent Comerford and Christian Noack. London, New York and Delhi: Anthem Press, 2012. 167–88. Print.

Kasianov, Georgiy. "Revisiting the Great Famine of 1932–1933: Politics of Memory and Public Consciousness (Ukraine after 1991)." *Past in the Making: Historical Revisionism and Central Europe after 1989*. Ed. Michal Kopeček. Budapest and New York: Central European University Press, 2008. 197–219. Print.

"Kil'kist' ukraintsiv, iaki vvazhaiiut' Holodomor henotsydom z kozhnym rokom zrostaie." *Tyzhden'* 11 Nov. 2013. Web. 24 Oct. 2014.

Kis, Oksana. "Defying Death: Women's Experience of the Holodomor, 1932–1933. *Aspasia* 7 (2013). Web. 1 June 2014.

Klid, Bohdan, and Alexander J. Motyl, eds. *The Holodomor Reader: A Sourcebook on the Famine of 1932–1933 in Ukraine*. Toronto: CIUS Press, 2012. Print.

Kocherha, Ol'ha. "Movoznavchi represii 1933 roku." *Ji* 35 (2004). Web. 24 Oct. 2014.

Kravchuk, Leonid. "My ne maiemo prava znekhtuvaty urokamy mynuloho." *Holodomor 1932–1933 rr. v Ukraini: prychyny ta naslidky*. Ed. Stanislav Kul'chyts'kyi. Kyiv: Instytut istorii, NAN Ukrainy, 1995. 8–11. Print.

Kul'chyts'kyi, Stanislav. "Dzheims Meis - liudyna i vchenyi." *Problemy istorii Ukrainy: fakty, sudzhennia, poshuky* 18 (2008): 9–28. Print.

---. "Holodomor 1932-33 rr.: Mekhanizm stalins'koho teroru." *Ukrains'kyi istorychnyi zhurnal* 4 (2007): 4–28. Print.

---. "Opir selianstva sutsil'nii kolektyvizatsii." *Holod 1932–1933 rokiv v Ukraini: Prychyny ta naslidky*. Ed. V. A. Smolii. Kyiv: Naukova dumka, 2003. Print.

---. *Pochemu on nas unichtozhal? Stalin i ukrainskii golodomor*. Kyiv: Ukrainskaia press-gruppa, 2007. Print.

---. *Ukrains'kyi Holodomor v konteksti polityky Kremlia pochatku 1930-x rr.* Kyiv: NAN Ukrainy, Instytut istorii Ukrainy, 2014. Print.

---. "'Vynyshchuval'ni aktsii': pam"iat' dvokh narodiv. Holodomory v Ukraini ta Kazakhstani u porivnial'nomu analizi (do pidsumkiv naukovoho seminaru v Kazakhstani)." *Den'* 30 May 2013. Web. 24 Oct. 2014.

Kulchytsky, Stanislav. "Why did Stalin exterminate the Ukrainians?" *The Day (Den')* 25 Oct. 2005; 1 Nov. 2005; 8 Nov. 2005; 15 Nov. 2005; 22 Nov. 2005. Web. 24 Oct. 2014.

Kuromiya, Hiroaki. *Freedom and Terror in the Donbas: A Ukrainian-Russian Borderland, 1870s–1990s*. Cambridge and New York: Cambridge University Press, 1998. Print.

---. *The Voices of the Dead: Stalin's Great Terror in the 1930s*. New Haven: Yale University Press, 2007. Print.

Lemkin, Raphael. *Axis Rule in Occupied Europe: Laws of Occupation, Analysis of Government, Proposals for Redress*. Washington: Carnegie Endowment for International Peace, Division of International Law, 1944. Print.

---. "Soviet Genocide in the Ukraine." *Holodomor: Reflections on the Great Famine of 1932–1933 in Soviet Ukraine*. Kingston: Kashtan Press, 2009. 235–42. Print.

Levchuk, N. M. "Raionna dyferentsiatsiia vtrat naselennia Ukrainy unaslidok holodu v 1933 rotsi." *Holod v Ukraini u pershii polovyni XX stolittia: Prychyny ta naslidky (1921–23, 1932–33, 1946–1947)*. Kyiv: Instytut istorii Ukrainy NAN Ukrainy, 2013. 257–64. Print.

Libanova, Ella. "Katastrofa ta ii vidlunnia: Otsinka demohrafichnykh vtrat Ukrainy vnaslidok Holodomoru 1932-33 rokiv." *Suchasnist'* 11 (2008): 22–29. Print.

---. "Otsinka demohrafichnykh vtrat Ukrainy vnaslidok Holodomoru 1932–1933 rokiv." *Holodomor 1932–1933 rokiv v Ukraini: prychyny, demohrafichni naslidky, pravova otsinka*. Kyiv: Kyievo-Mohylians'ka akademiia, 2009. 266–77. Print.

Lih, Lars T., Oleg V. Naumov, and Oleg V. Khlevniuk, eds. *Stalin's Letters to Molotov*. New Haven: Yale University Press, 1995. Print.

Maniak, Volodymyr A., and Lidiia B. Kovalenko, eds. *"33-i Holod": Narodna Knyha - Memorial*. Kyiv: Radians'kyi pys'mennyk, 1991. Print.

Martin, Terry. *The Affirmative Action Empire: Nations and Nationalism in the Soviet Union, 1923–1939*. Ithaca: Cornell University Press, 2001. Print.

Matvieiev, A. Iu. *Kolektyvizatsiia i rozkurkulennia selian Podillia ta Pivdenno-Skhidnoi Volyni (druha polovyna 20-kh - seredyna 30-kh rokiv XX st.)*. Chernivtsi: Chernivets'kyi natsional'nyi universytet im. Iu. Fed'kovycha, 2009. Print.

McDonnell, Michael A., and A. Dirk Moses. "Raphael Lemkin as Historian of Genocide in the Americas." *Journal of Genocide Research* 7.4 (December 2005): 501–29. Print.

Motyl, Alexander J. "Deleting the Holodomor: Ukraine Unmakes Itself." *World Affairs Journal*. September/October 2010. Web. 24 Oct. 2014.

---. "Ukraine's Orange Blues: Genocide's Definition Revisited." *World Affairs Journal*. 19 Oct. 2012. Web. 24 Oct. 2014.

---. "Ukraine's Orange Blues: Was the Holodomor Genocide?" *World Affairs Journal*. 8 Apr. 2011. Web. 24 Oct. 2014.

---. "Ukraine's Orange Blues: Yanukovych and Stalin's Genocide." *World Affairs Journal*. 29 Nov. 2012. Web. 24 Oct. 2014.

Natsional'na Knyha pam"iati zhertv Holodomoru 1932–1933 rr. v Ukraini. 19 vols. Kyiv: Ukrains'kyi instytut natsionalnoi pam"iati, 2008. Print.

Noll, Vil'iam. *Transformatsiia hromadians'koho suspil'stva. Usna istoriia selians'koi kul'tury 1920–30 rokiv*. Kyiv: Rodovid, 1999. Print.

Odynoka, L. P., L. F. Prykhod'ko, and R. V. Romanovs'kyi, eds. *Holodomory v Ukraini 1921–23, 1932–1933, 1946–1947*. Kyiv: Derzhavnyi komitet arkhiviv Ukrainy, Ukrains'kyi naukovo-doslidnyi instytut arkhivnoi spravy ta dokumentoznavstva, 2005. Print.

Papakin, H. "'Blacklists' as a Tool of the Soviet Genocide in Ukraine." *Holodomor Studies* 1.1 (2009): 55–75. Print.

Papakin, Heorhii. "Arkhivni dokumenty pro 'Chorni doshky' iak znariaddia radians'koho henotsydu v Ukraini v 1932–1933 rokakh." *Arkhivy Ukrainy* 261.3–4 (2008): 14–28. Print.

---. *'Chorna doshka': antyselians'ki represii (1932–33)*. Kyiv: Instytut istorii Ukrainy, 2013. Print.

---. "'Chorni doshky' Holodomoru—ekonomichnyi metod znyshchennia hromadian URSR." *Ukrains'ka pravda* 27 November 2010. Web. 24 Oct. 2014.

---. "'Chorni doshky' iak oblychchia Holodomoru." Web. 24 Oct. 2014. <http://histans.com/LiberUA/Papakin_Bl_Desk/Papakin_Bl_Desk.pdf>

---. "'Chorni doshky' iak znariaddia radians'koho henotsydu v Ukraini v 1932–1933 rokakh." *Holodomor 1932–1933 rokiv v Ukraini: prychyny, demohrafichni naslidky, pravova otsinka*. Ukrains'kyi instytut natsional'noi pam'iati. Kyiv: Akademiia, 2009. 59–87. Print.

---. "Neopublikovani stalins'ki dyrektyvy lystopada 1932 r.: Kreml' i 'chorna doshka'." *Ukrains'kyi istorychnyi zhurnal* 6 (2013): 45–57. Print.

Papakin, Heorhii, and Olena Lisniak. "Dodatok: Zahal'nyi spysok naselenykh punktiv, zanesenykh na 'chornu doshku' u 1932–1933 rr." *Institut Istorii Ukrainy, Natsional'na Akademii Nauk Ukrainy* (2010). Web. 24 Oct. 2014. <http://www.history.org.ua/index.php?litera&id=9033&navStart=3>

Petrenko, Ie. D. "Ukrains'ke kozatstvo v ostanii chverti XVIII - na pochatku XX st." *Problemy istorii Ukrainy XIX - pochatku XX st.* 15 (2008): 129–33. Print.

Pidhainy, Semen, ed. *The Black Deeds of the Kremlin: A White Book*. Vol. I. Toronto: Ukrainian Association of Victims of Russian Communist Terror, 1953; Vol. II. Detroit:

Democratic Organization of Ukrainians Formerly Persecuted by the Soviet Regime, 1955. Print.

"Polovyna zhyteliv skhidnoi Ukrainy zaperechuiut', shcho Holodomor buv henotsydom." *Dzerkalo tyzhnia* 21 November 2012. Web. 24 Oct. 2014.

Postyshev, P. "Borot'ba KP(b)U za zdiisnennia lenins'koi natsional'noi polityky na Ukraini." *Chervonyi shliakh* 2-3 (1934): 165-76. Print.

Pshenychnyi, Taras Iu. *Holod 1932-1933 rokiv v Ukraini (na materialakh pivdenno-skhidnykh oblastei)*. Pereiaslav-Khmelnyts'kyi: Pereiaslav-Khmel'nyts'kyi derzh. pedahohichnyi universytet im. Hryhoriia Skovorody, 2008. Print.

Pyrih, R. Ia., ed. *Holodomor. 1932-1933 v Ukraini: dokumenty i materialy*. Kyiv: Kyievo-Mohylians'ka Akademiia, 2007. Print.

Rudnyts'kyi, O. P., and A. B. Savchuk. "Holod 1932-33 rr. v Ukraini u demohrafichnomu vymiri." *Holod v Ukraini u pershii polovyni XX stolittia: Prychyny ta naslidky (1921-23, 1932-33, 1946-47)*. Kyiv: Instytut istorii Ukrainy NAN Ukrainy, 2013. 281-88. Print.

Rudnytsky, O., et al. "1932-33 Famine Losses in Ukraine within the Context of the Soviet Union." *Famines in European Economic History: The Last Great European Famines Reconsidered*. Ed. Declan Curran, Lubomyr Luciuk and Andrew Newby. London and New York: Routledge, forthcoming 2015. Print.

"SBU nazvala ostatochnu kil'kist' zhertv Holodomoru v Ukraini." *TSN*. 14 Jan. 2010. Web. 24 Oct. 2014.

Scott, James C. *Seeing Like a State: How Certain Schemes to Improve the Human Condition Have Failed*. Yale Agrarian Studies. New Haven, Conn.: Yale UP, 1998. Print.

Serbyn, Roman. "Is There a 'Smoking Gun' for the Holodomor?" *UNIAN*. 19 Nov. 2007. Web. 24 Oct. 2014.

---. "Osmyslennia Holodomoru v svitli konventsii OON pro genotsyd." *Holodomor 1932-1933: prychyny, demohrafichni naslidyky, pravova otsinka*. Kyiv: Kyievo-Mohylians'ka Akademiia, 2009. 400-412. Print.

---. "Raphael Lemkin, the UN Convention of 1948, and the Case for the Ukrainian Genocide." Danyliw Research Seminar in Contemporary Ukrainian Studies. *Yumpu*. 2008. Web. 24 Oct. 2014.

---. "The Ukrainian Famine of 1932-1933 as Genocide in the Light of the UN Convention of 1948." *The Ukrainian Quarterly* 62 (2): 181-94. Print.

Serbyn, Roman, and Bohdan Krawchenko, eds. *Famine in Ukraine 1932-1933*. Edmonton: Canadian Institute of Ukrainian Studies, 1986. Print.

Serbyn, Roman, and Olesia Stasiuk, eds. *Rafael' Lemkin: Riadians'kyi henotsyd v Ukraini (stattia 28 movamy)*. Kyiv: Maisternia knyhy, 2009. Print.

Serput'ko, Alla Iuriivna. "Suchasna ukrainsk'ka ta rosiis'ka istoriohrafiia prychyn ta naslidkiv holodomoru v URSR 1932-1933 rokiv." Kand. ist. nauk. Cherkasy. Natsional'nyi universytet im. B. Khmel'nyts'koho, 2009. Print.

Shevchuk, P. Ie. "Metodychni pidkhody do obchyslennia demohrafichnykh utrat pid chas holodu 1932-33 rr." *Holod v Ukraini u pershii polovyni XX stolittia: Prychyny ta naslidky (1921-23, 1932-33, 1946-1947)*. Kyiv: Instytut istorii Ukrainy NAN Ukrainy, 2013. 289-93. Print.

Soldatenko, V. F. [Valerii F.] "Prychyny ta demohrafichni naslidky holodu 1932-1933 rr.: dva pohliady na odne iavyshche (do 79-oi richnytsi Holodomoru 1932-33 rokiv)." *Ukrains'kyi Instytut Natsional'noi pam'iati* (2012). Web. 5 Sept. 2013. <http://histans.com/LiberUA/PrNasl/PrNasl.pdf>

---. "Trahediia trydtsiat' tret'oho: notatky na istoriohrafichnomu zrizi." *Natsional'na ta istorychna pam"iat': zbirnyk naukovykh prats'*. Kyiv: Ukrains'kyi instytut natsional'noi pam"iati, 2012. 3–92. Print.

---. "Ukrains'kyi instytut national'noi pam"iati s'ohodni." *Ukrains'kyi instytut natsional'noi pam"iati* (2014). Web. 24 Oct. 2014. <http://www.memory.gov.ua/news/ukrainskii-institut-natsionalnoi-pam-yati-sogodni>

Solovei, D. F. [Dmytro F.] *Skazaty pravdu: try pratsi pro holodomor 1932–1933 rokiv*. Kyiv and Poltava: [n.p.], 2005. Print.

Solvey, Dmytro. *The Golgotha of Ukraine*. New York: Ukrainian Congress Committee of America, 1953. Print.

Starovoitov, Mykola M., and Volodymyr V. Mykhailychenko, eds. *Holodomor na Luhanshchyni 1932–1933 rr.: Naukovo-dokumental'ne vydannia*. Kyiv: Stylos, 2008. Print.

Stasiuk, Olesia. "Deformatsiia narodnoi kul'tury v roky henotsydu." *Problemy istorii Ukrainy: fakty, sudzhennia, poshuky* 18 (2008): 349–61. Print.

---. *Henotsyd ukraintsiv: deformatsiia narodnoi kul'tury*. Kyiv: Stylos, 2008. Print.

Sukhomlin, Nikolai. "Ukraina vtratyla vid holodomoru ponad 10 mil'ioniv osib." *KhaiVei* 23 December 2009. Web. 24 Oct. 2014.

Suslyk, L. R. *Sumni spohady: 1933 rik na Poltavshchyni*. Munich?: [n.p.], 1951. Print.

Sysyn, Frank. "The Ukrainian Famine of 1932–3: The Role of the Ukrainian Diaspora in Research and Public Discussion." *Studies in Comparative Genocide*. Ed. Levron Chorbajian and George Shirinian. New York-London: Palgrave Macmillan, 1999. 182–215. Print.

"Ukaz Prezydenta Ukrainy № 1310/98 Pro vstanovlennia Dnia pam"iati zhertv holodomoriv ta politychnyk represii." *president.gov.ua*. 26 Nov. 1998. Web. 24 Oct. 2014.

"Ukaz Prezydenta Ukrainy No. 868/2006. Pro vidznachennia u 2006 rotsi Dnia pam"iati zhertv holodomoriv ta politychnykh represii." *Verkhovna rada Ukrainy*. 12 Oct. 2006. Web. 24 Oct. 2014.

"Ukaz Prezydenta Ukrainy № 431/2007. Pro zakhody u zv"iazku z 70-my rokovynamy Velykoho teroru - masovykh politychnykh represii 1937 – 1938 rokiv." *president.gov.ua*. 21 May 2007. Web. 24 Oct. 2014.

United States. Commission on the Ukraine Famine. *Investigation of the Ukrainian Famine, 1932–1933: Report to Congress*. Washington: U.S. G.P.O., 1988. Print.

Vallin, Jacques, et al. "A New Estimate of Ukrainian population losses during the crises of the 1930s and 1940s. *Population Studies* 56 (2002): 249–64. Print.

Vallin, Jacques, et al. "The Great Famine: Population Losses in Ukraine." *Demohrafiia ta sotsial'na ekonomika* 2.12 (2009): 3–11. Print.

Vasil'ev, Valerii. "Krest'ianskie vosstaniia na Ukraine: 1929–1930 gody." *Svobodnaia mysl'*, 1992, no. 9: 70–78. Print.

Vasyl'iev, Valerii. "Evoliutsiia pohliadiv S. Kul'chyts'koho na holod 1932–1933 rr. u konteksti novitnykh tendentsii ukrains'koi istoriohrafii." *Problemy istorii Ukrainy: fakty, sudzhennia, poshuky* 16.1 (2007): 277–86. Print.

---. "Osoblyvosti vidnosyn Kremlia z kerivnytstvom riadians'koi Ukrainy pid chas Holodomoru 1932–1933 rr." *Taking Measure of the Holodomor*. New York: The Center for U.S.-Ukrainian Relations, 2013. Web. 24 Oct. 2014. <http:

//usukrainianrelations.org/index.php?option=com_content&task=view&id=36 6&Itemid=206>
---. "Porivnial'nyi analiz holodu ta Holodomoru: Vinnyts'ka oblast' (1920-1940-i rr.)." *Istoriia Ukrainy: Malovidomi imena, podii, fakty* 37 (2011): 111-35. Print.
---. "Selians'kyi opir kolektyvizatsii v Ukraini (1930-ti rr.)." *Istoriia Ukrainy: Malovidomi imena, podii, fakty* 31 (2005): 140-50. Print.
---. "Stosunky kerivnytstva SRSR ta USRR u 1932-1933 rokakh: 'Kryza doviry'." *Holodomor 1932-1933 rokiv v Ukraini: prychyny, demohrafichni naslidky, pravova otsinka*. Kyiv: Kyievo-Mohylians'ka akademiia, 2009. 87-108. Print.
Vasyl'iev, V., and Iu. Shapoval, eds. *Komandyry velykoho holodu: Poizdka V. Molotova i L. Kaganovycha v Ukrainu ta na Pivnichnyi Kavkaz 1932-1933 rr.* Kyiv: Geneza, 2001. Print.
Vasyl'iev, V., N. Vert, and S. Kokin, eds. *Partiino-radians'ke kerivnytstvo USRR pid chas Holodomoru 1932-1933 rr.: Vozhdi. Pratsivnyky. Aktyvisty. Zbirnyk dokumentiv ta materialiv*. Kyiv: Instytut istorii Ukrainy, 2013. Print.
Verstiuk, Vladyslav. "Ukrains'ko-rosiis'ki vidnosyny u sferi doslidzhennia pytan' Holodomoru 1932-1933 rr." *Problemy istorii Ukrainy: fakty, sudzhennia, poshuky* 18 (2008): 228-31. Print.
Veselova, Oleksandra. "Do problemy henotsydu ukrains'koho narodu holodom 1932-1933 rr." *Problemy istorii Ukrainy: fakty, sudzhennia, poshuky* 18 (2008): 101-12. Print.
---. "Holod iak viddzerkalennia represyvnoi polityky totalitarnoi imperii." *Holodomory v Ukraini, 1921-1923, 1932-1933, 1946-1947: Zlochyny proty narodu*. Ed. O. Veselova, V. I. Marochko, and O. M. Movchan. Kyiv and New York: Vydavnytstvo M.P. Kots', 2000. 188-212. Print.
---. "Pam"iatni znaky i pam"iatnyky zhertvam Holodu-henotsydu 1932-1933 v Ukraini." *Problemy istorii Ukrainy: fakty, sudzhennia, poshuky* 13 (2005): 434-41. Print.
---. "Svidchennia ochevydtsiv holodu-henotsydu 1932-1933 rokiv v Ukraini iak dzherelo vyvchennia ioho prychyn i naslidkiv." *Holodomor 1932-1933 rokiv v Ukraini: prychyny, demohrafichni naslidky, pravova otsinka*. Kyiv: Kyievo-Mohylians'ka akademiia, 2009. 189-210. Print.
Veselova, O., V. I. Marochko, and O. M. Movchan, eds. *Holodomory v Ukraini, 1921-1923, 1932-1933, 1946-1947: Zlochyny proty narodu*. Kyiv and New York: Vydavnytstvo M.P. Kots', 2000. Print.
Viedienieiev, D. V., and D. V. Budkov. *Zaruchnytsia hlobal'noho protystoiannia: Trahediia Velykoho Holodu 1932-1933 rr. v Ukraini v konteksti "kholodnoi viiny" (1945-1991 rr.)*. Kyiv: Dorado-Druk, 2013. Print.
Viola, Lynne. *Peasant Rebels Under Stalin: Collectivization and the Culture of Peasant Resistance*. New York: Oxford University Press, 1996. Print.
"Vitse-prem"ier ministr Ukrainy Oleskandr Sych predstavyv kolektyvu Ukrains'koho instytutu natsional'noi pam"iati novoho dyrektora - Volodymyra V'iatrovycha." *Ukrains'kyi instytut natsional'noi pam"iati*. 27 March 2014. Web. 14 Apr. 2014.
Volovyna [Wolowyna], Oleh. "Pomisiachnyi rozpodil demohrafichnykh vtrat vnaslidok holodu 1933 roku v Ukraini." *Holod v Ukraini u pershii polovyni XX stolittia: prychyny ta naslidky (1921-23, 1932-33, 1946-1947)*. Kyiv: Instytut istorii Ukrainy NAN Ukrainy, 2013. 233-42. Print.

von Hagen, Mark. "Rethinking the Meaning of the Holodomor: 'Notes and Materials' toward a(n) (Anti) (Post) Colonial History of Ukraine." *Taking Measure of the Holodomor*. New York: The Center for U.S.-Ukrainian Relations, 2013. Web. 24 Oct. 2014. <http://usukrainianrelations.org/images/pdf/[HESSE 201] von Hagen-Rethinking the Meaning of the Holodomor.pdf>

Werth, Nicolas. "The Great Ukrainian Famine of 1932–33." *Online Encyclopedia of Mass Violence* 2008. Web. 24 Oct. 2014.

Wheatcroft, S. G. "Mapping Crude Death Rates in Ukraine in 1933 and Explaining the Raion Patterns." *Holod v Ukraini u pershii polovyni XX stolittia: prychyny ta naslidky (1921–23, 1932–33, 1946–1947)*. Kyiv: Instytut istorii Ukrainy NAN Ukrainy, 2013. 219–25. Print.

Wolowyna, Oleh. "The Famine-Genocide of 1932–33: Estimation of Losses and Demographic Impact." *The Holodomor Reader: A Sourcebook on the Famine of 1932–1933 in Ukraine*. Ed. Bohdan Klid and Alexander J. Motyl. Toronto: CIUS Press, 2012. 59–64. Print.

---. "Holodomor Losses: Methodological Problems and Research Challenges." *Holodomor 1932–1933 rokiv v Ukraini: prychyny, demohrafichni naslidky, pravova otsinka*. Kyiv: Kyievo-Mohylians'ka akademiia, 2009. 278–92. Print.

"Yanukovych Reverses Ukraine's Position on Holodomor Famine." *RIA Novosti*. 27 April 2010. Web. 24 Oct. 2014.

"Zakon Ukrainy pro Holodomor 1932–1933 v Ukraini." *Vidomosti Verkhovnoi Rady Ukrainy* 50 (2006): 504. Print.

Zawada, Zenon "Wikileaks and Ukraine: Holodomor, Shady Business Deals and Gaddafi." *The Ukrainian Weekly* 5 December 2010: 1, 19. Print.

Zymovets', Roman. "Kam"iani kozats'ki khresty ta sil's'ki tsvyntari Trakhtemyrivs'koho rehionu: malovidomi memorial'ni pam"iatky ukrains'koi istorii." *Arkheolohiia Seredn'oi Naddniprianshchyny*. 16 June 2013. Web. 24 Oct. 2014.

The Impact of Holodomor Studies on the Understanding of the USSR

Andrea Graziosi
University of Naples Federico II

Abstract: This paper investigates what the Holodomor tells us about the development and dynamics of Soviet history. It begins with an examination of the evolving relations between Stalin and the peasantry during the first decades of the Soviet Union as well as the social, economic, moral, and psychological consequences following the destruction of traditional rural society in the USSR. The relationship between the Holodomor and the viability of the Soviet system is discussed along with the opportunities that history presented to the Soviet leadership after 1945 to reverse the country's critical 1928-29 decisions. This leadership's awareness of the tragedies of the 1930s in the countryside and their consequences are raised before shifting the focus to the linkage between the peasant and the national questions in Soviet history. In this context the Holodomor is discussed as a tool to solve both the peasant and the national "irritants" caused by Ukraine to both the Soviet system and Stalin's personal power. The legacy of this "solution" is addressed, including consideration of the background of the collapse of the Soviet system from the perspective of the sustainability of a state whose past is tainted by unacknowledged genocidal practices. The paper ends with a discussion of the consequences of the growing awareness of the importance of the Holodomor and the impact on the image of the USSR, and in particular, the question of the "modernity" of the Soviet system and of the "modernizing" effects of Stalin's 1928-29 policies.

Keywords: Holodomor, USSR, Genocide, Stalinism, Peasantry, National Question

This paper assesses the impact of the Holodomor on our understanding of Soviet history and reflects upon what the Famine and its legacy tell us about the development and dynamics of this history and of Ukrainian history. It begins with a discussion of how that history appears if one assigns the Holodomor—along with collectivization and the civil war—a proper role. From this perspective, the evolution of relations between Stalin and his regime with the peasantry prove crucial to understanding the first decades of the Soviet Union.

Several issues will be addressed: the viability of the Soviet system in relation to the collective system that the Famine forced upon the country, and the opportunities that history presented to the Soviet leadership after the Second World War victory—and then again after Stalin's death—to change the decisions of 1928-29 regarding collectivization (with a comparison to Deng Xiaoping's reforms in China). I will discuss the Soviet ruling elite's awareness of, and attitudes toward, the tragedies of the 1930s in the countryside and their consequences. The weight of the illusions regarding the potential of collectivized agriculture and of the taboo Stalin successfully imposed upon the famines will be analyzed in connection with the structural limits of the post-1953 reforms and the economic and social degradation of the system they were unable to change.

I shall deal with the close linkage between the peasant and the national questions in Soviet history, of which Ukraine was the paramount case, especially in Stalin's reckoning. In this context, the Holodomor will be discussed as a tool that dealt with, in one stroke, both the peasant and the national "irritants" to the Soviet system and Stalin's personal power, given Ukraine's relative autonomy. The legacy of the solution—for example, in the realm of language and culture—will be addressed. I will, in short, return to the question of the collapse of the Soviet system from yet another perspective, i.e., that of the viability of a state and system whose past is marred by an unacknowledged genocide, possibly more than one. Finally, I will turn to the consequences that the growing awareness of the importance and nature of the Holodomor have had on the image of the USSR and its representation by historians. In particular, the "modernity" of the Soviet system and of the "modernizing" effects of Stalin's 1928–29 policies will be raised.

This paper is based on my personal experience as a historian of the USSR and my participation in the extraordinary period of research into Soviet history in the wake of the collapse of the Soviet Union in 1991. In 1986–87 my examination of Italian diplomatic dispatches forced me to confront the Holodomor. They made for painful reading, but I was immediately aware that my understanding of Soviet history and of the twentieth century in Europe was going to be radically altered. The impact of these reports was furthered by the admittedly partial but substantial opening of Soviet archives and by the documents emerging from them. Among them, the most notable were the following:

a. The Cheka/OGPU operational summaries (*svodki*) on state-peasant relations during the civil war;[1]

---

[1] I was given the reports to prepare an introduction to the first volume (1918–22) of the series *Sovetskaia derevnia glazami VChK-OGPU-NKVD, 1918–1939*. However, the editor, V. P. Danilov, refused to publish my text because—by my extending to the Soviet period a concept he had developed for the late Tsarist period—it spoke of a war against the peasantry as key to understanding Soviet history and thus was too

b. Materials on the revolts by Ukrainian villages against de-kulakization and collectivization that I found in the Ordzhonikidze secret archive and the OGPU *svodki* on the 1930-33 countryside;
c. The large body of documentation, testimonies and scholarship on the Holodomor and the 1931-34 famines—but also on the 1920-22 and the 1946-47 ones—that became increasingly available after the collapse of the USSR; and
d. The documents selected for the multi-volume series *Dokumenty sovetskoi istorii*, which started to appear in Moscow in 1993 under the supervision of Oleg Khlevniuk and myself.

In dealing with these questions, I could not but rely on my previous writings. Readers will find there a more detailed treatment of events and problems, summarized here in an effort to examine the impact of the Holodomor on Soviet history and our understanding of it.[2]

1. THE PEASANT QUESTION IN SOVIET HISTORY

The Holodomor—and the other famines that accompanied and followed it, beginning with the civil war and continuing through Stalin's death—highlight the opposition to the new state by different "peasantries," which I refer to as the Great Soviet Peasant War of 1918-1934. This is fundamental to understanding the history of the first decades of the USSR.

This acknowledgement has a devastating impact on more traditional interpretations: the "workerist" rhetoric—in all of its variants, both pro- and anti-regime[3]—appears, precisely, only as rhetoric, with little relevance

---

"anti-Soviet." The materials he continued to publish eventually convinced him to espouse a similar view, which I had meanwhile formalized in Graziosi, *Great Soviet Peasant War*.

[2] The reader is referred, in particular, to: "The Great Famine of 1932-33"; "Vneshniaia i vnutrennaia politika Stalina"; "Stalin, krest'ianstvo i gosudarstvennyi socializm"; *L'Urss di Lenin e Stalin*; *L'Urss dal trionfo al degrado* (an abridged edition of the two volumes has been published in France by the Presses Universitaires de France in 2010 and is also forthcoming from Rosspen in Moscow); and "Stalin's Genocides, and...?".

[3] The former started from the early Stalinist presentation of Soviet history as a heroic process, led by a workers' party, of building a worker state, to later readings that, while not denying the great suffering of the 1930s, presented them as necessary for the construction of socialism. The latter was supported initially by former oppositionists, who presented the Stalinist state as a perversion of the "true" worker state. It was revived after 1991 by archival findings about the intense

for the dynamics of Soviet history. Various "modernization" theories and interpretations that construct a particularly Soviet "welfare state" do not fare any better. If we look back from 1931 to 1934, we see the following:

a. From the spring of 1918 onward and through de-kulakization, collectivization and the famines, "classes" had but a marginal (although certainly not non-existent) role in what was basically an original, ideologically inspired, very violent and primitive state-building attempt. In this process, individual leaders (and their psychologies and mentalities), state and Party bureaucracies, and even common criminals played crucial roles[4];

b. Peasant opposition to this kind of state-building and the role of the peasants in supporting national liberation movements, as in 1919 Ukraine, were also crucial in the affirmation of those indigenization policies (*korenizatsiia*) that represented one of the Soviet Union's most important and original features. Their fate—most notably but not exclusively in Ukraine—was to be determined by developments in the state-peasantry confrontation in the early 1930s;

c. The previous two points are confirmed by the substantial and impressive geographical, ideological, and even personal and "family" continuity between the peasant-based social and national revolts of 1918–20 and those against de-kulakization, requisitions, and collectivization in 1930–31. Remarks by Vsevolod Balyts'kyi in 1930 and Kliment Voroshilov in 1934 prove that Soviet leaders were keenly aware of this continuity, which was strongest in territories where famine reached its harshest peaks in 1931–34, particularly the regions between Kyiv and Kharkiv (the data collected by the Harvard Ukrainian Research Institute for its Digital Atlas of Ukraine are in this regard quite impressive) as well as the Kuban, the Don and Volga regions, and Central Asia.

If we now try instead to look from 1933 forward, thus entering less thoroughly studied territory, we can observe the following:

---

repression the regime carried out in factories already during the civil war and later, especially after 1927.

[4] The criminal element was very relevant in the formation of the most violent of those very bureaucracies, a fact that the Cheka/GPU reports repeatedly note and that is now also being stressed by students of other great state-led twentieth-century transformative projects.

a. The powerful impact that the famine experience—which included harrowing personal suffering, extreme survival strategies (even cannibalism), and devastating mourning—had on peasant behaviour, psychologies, mentalities, and even religion. About ten years ago, I raised the question of the legacy for the population of those several months in which millions died. What, for example, was the impact of depression, which struck rural families that could not mourn their dead and were deprived of religious and other authorities who might have help them cope with their grief (Graziosi, "Great Famine" 157-60)? Unfortunately, we lack a social history "from-below" of the Ukrainian Famine, as lived and seen by peasants—this being in my judgment the new frontier for Holodomor studies. We do have torturing glimpses of it in numerous eyewitness accounts, in the trials for cannibalism, and in GPU documents, which raise most gripping questions about individual and collective behaviours as well as beliefs inspired by collectivization and hunger.[5]

b. The increased role alcohol played as a consequence of both the peasants' and the state's behaviour. Relying on old habits that the civil war and the 1921-22 famine had strengthened, peasants in the 1930s increased their consumption of alcohol to escape extreme hardships, depression, and everyday misery. Meanwhile the Soviet state—looking for money—made sure that alcohol was available in increasing quantities and without competition in country stores. We know that already in the mid-1920s Stalin had justified the increase in the production and sale of vodka as a way to find funds needed for industrialization. The crisis provoked by

---

[5] For instance, a GPU report from Vinnytsia, dated January 1934, deals with the illegal religious services held for victims of famine, which had multiplied in previous months and were accompanied by rumours about miracles. "Two strangers carrying icons" had entered a village "saying that in a nearby hamlet a person claiming to have been resuscitated from death by starvation urged believers, and women who had not joined collective farms in particular, to organize wakes to remember the famine victims. If such wakes were organized, God would have forgiven the people's sins. Otherwise an even worse famine would have come, which noone would have survived." According to the report, hundreds of people, including different kinds of formerly repressed people (such as previously deported peasants), joined such gatherings, which sent delegations to surrounding villages. "Operational detachments were however dispatched to the infected districts, and orders were given to all OGPU organs in order to stop the phenomenon." See Werth and Berelowitch 554.

the "great offensive" he launched in 1929 made things even worse. On 1 September 1930, while official rhetoric extolled the new "Soviet man," Stalin wrote to Molotov, "I think vodka production should be expanded *(to the extent possible)*. We need to get rid of a false sense of shame and directly and openly expand as much as possible the production of vodka for the sake of the real and serious defense of our country" (Lih et al. 209; Khlevniuk 209). Thus for the first time Soviet vodka production surpassed that of the much larger Tsarist empire, and vodka came to represent up to 40 percent of the total sales of rural stores and to provide about 20 percent of state revenues (Hessler 164; Graziosi, *L'URSS di Lenin e Stalin* 300ff). The new regime thus became a pusher of narcotics to an alien and destitute population, and also in this way caused the ruin of traditional peasant and human culture.

c. What Sergei Maksudov rightly calls dehumanization *(raschelovechivanie)*, that is, the "change in the moral and ethical consciousness of the Soviet citizens as a result of collectivization and famine."[6] This transformation became an important dimension of what Krasil'nikov has termed Stalin's repressive de-peasantization *(repressivnoe raskrest'ianivanie)*. Among other things, these phenomena caused the appearance—especially in the countryside—of a "new human being" who "was passive, meekly carried out even the most absurd instructions of the authorities, was ready to work for the lowest wage or even for free, did not like and did not respect his own work, lacked confidence, feared the unexpected, if he could, did not obey laws, considered theft the natural form of the redistribution of property, and did not feel self-respect" (Krasil'nikov 44-55).[7]

In the long run these processes left a legacy represented by the terrible social and psychological conditions of rural Soviet settlements, whose "death" the "village writers" *(derevenshchiki)* had started to describe in their novels already at the beginning of the 1950s (Valentin Ovechkin's *Raionnye budni* being one of the best examples). Above all, they contributed to the peculiar dynamics of Soviet demographic evolution. As Meslé and Vallin (among others) have demonstrated, alcoholism and psychological deprivation had an impact on life expectancy—that of men in particular (Meslé and Vallin). The Soviet leaders' awareness of its dramatic effects was

---

[6] The description of "dehumanization" is found in the subtitle to Maksudov.

[7] Needless to say, not everyone possessed such features, and those who did, possessed them in varying degrees.

to play an important role in igniting the reform efforts of the 1980s, thereby accelerating the demise of the Soviet system.

2. The Holodomor and the Viability of the Soviet System

The Holodomor casts its shadow on yet another of the major questions pertaining to the viability of the Soviet system, namely, its agricultural policy. Stalin forced collectivization down the throats of peasants by a Pavlovian use of hunger; the peasants immediately recognized it as a "second serfdom." According to Anatoly Chernyaev, in the 1980s even the General Secretary of the Party—unaware of the GPU reports that recorded such opinions from fifty or so years earlier—"scornfully" called the collective farms (*kolkhozy* or *kolhospy*) an "unshakable" servile system run by "*kolkhoz* generals" (Chernyaev 216). But by making it possible to impose a new kind of serfdom on the countryside, the Holodomor and the Soviet famines also established the structural foundations of the agricultural crisis that marked Soviet history from the time of Stalin's "revolution from above." By the 1970s it had reached unsustainable proportions.

This crisis was the direct consequence of the system that emerged from the peasants' defeat and from that of "peasant" nations, of which Ukraine was in Stalin's eyes by far the most important. Once hunger ensured such defeats and the stabilization of the collective farm system, Stalin was forced to introduce two measures that temporarily saved what remained of the peasants and peasant culture, yet at the same time profoundly deformed them. The end of rationing and the introduction of the "*kolkhozian* market," which allowed peasants to shop and sell in cities, were a major relief for the villages (Davies and Khlevniuk 87–108). But the most important measure was the right granted to *kolkhozniki* in 1935 to cultivate a small personal plot (0.2-0.5 hectare), the so-called *lichnoe podsobnoe khoziaistvo* (LPKh). *Kolkhozniki* could thus continue to be mini-*muzhiki* on the side (Lewin 186–87), and the terrible de-peasantization of the early part of the decade ended up generating a system that preserved at its core a mini-peasant who was fated to slowly fade away in subsequent years, after providing the country with new flesh and blood during the war and the post-war "modernization."

Together with the establishment of the collective farm system, these two measures defined the new rural economic system. Initially, this meant the ability to buy and sell as well as exploit plots, which improved the conditions of collective farm workers. Yet even though this ameliorated the situation (not a difficult task, given the misery that had prevailed in the countryside since 1928), the new system also pulled in opposite directions. As attested to by his speech at the March 1935 *kolkhoz* conference (*Pravda* 15 March 1935), Stalin was perfectly aware of the situation:

> If in your artels you don't yet have food in abundance and can't give to the collective farmer and his family everything that they need, the *kolkhoz* can't take it upon itself to satisfy both public and private needs. In that case it would be better to say directly that this sphere is public, and that one is private. It would be better to admit frankly, openly and honestly that a collective farm household should have a private plot, not a big one, but private. It's better to proceed from the fact that there is an artel, public, large, social, and decisive, necessary to meet public needs, and there is alongside it a small, private farm, necessary to meet the needs of the collective farmer. As long as there is family, children, private needs and private tastes, you can't fail to pay attention to them. And you don't have the right to ignore the personal interests of collective farmers. Without this, the consolidation of the *kolkhoz* is impossible.

The divergent interests regulating these two spheres of endeavor doomed them both to atrophy. The "big, social, decisive" sector generated a lack of interest on the part of collective farm labourers since everybody knew, and official proclamations openly stated, that its production belonged to the state. The waning of the LPKh was pre-determined by its miniscule dimensions and by the vigilance exerted by the state to prevent it from growing (and to limit its productivity) in the fear that the mini-*muzhik* would devote most of his time to his plot.

The state was thus adamantly opposed to the development of the private sector, and the collective farmers were poised against that of the social one. A letter that the peasants of a Ural collective farm mailed in 1938 to local authorities clearly stated:

> Collective farms... function first and foremost as agents of political-economic campaigns. Their administrations operate—even if not always satisfactorily—as tools of superior organizations entrusted with fulfillment of plans of food procurement for the state and other tasks set by the plan. Collective farms as of now do not perform well enough to convince the population that their purpose is to raise the standard of living of collective farmers.... The conditions of collective farms... appear as if designed to instill in the population the idea that it would be better to return to capitalism. Such conditions could be produced by the enemies of the people. (Graziosi, *L'Urss di Lenin e Stalin* 394 ff.; see also Beznin and Dimoni; Beznin, Dimoni and Iziumova; Kessler and Kornilov; Popov)

Not surprisingly, as we can read in yet another document, already by 1939, "most collective farm workers... turn their private plot into their main concern, and the *kolkhoz* fields into subsidiary activities, and evade participation in social work" (Kessler and Kornilov 111–15). The state considered such behaviour a crime and it was punished as such. To assure their survival, peasants reacted by devising all sorts of schemes, including pilfering, which hunger had made an everyday necessity (Fitzpatrick 57, 65–67, 72–73). This amounted to the destruction of the previous peasant way of life (*byt*), whose moral and economic pillars had already started to disintegrate under the impact of de-kulakization, collectivization and hunger, growing alcohol consumption, and the ban on religion.

Even though potentially capable of guaranteeing both the survival of the peasantry and the transfer to the state of the bulk of agricultural production, the 1935 "compromise" that the state was able to enforce (following its victory through hunger) provided Soviet agriculture and Soviet society in general with a fragile basis for food procurement. It was to remain one of the weakest points of the system until its final collapse, to which the "compromise" certainly contributed.

The difficulties of the transition to a communist future were summed up in Stalin's *Ekonomicheskie problemy sotsializma v SSSR* (Economic Problems of Socialism in the USSR, 1952), showing that he too realized that the agricultural system that emerged from the 1929–33 catastrophe was in a quagmire. Significantly, he attributed the problem to the collective farms, whose very existence precluded the abolition of the "law of value." This was so because *kolkhozy* were cooperatives owned by peasants, who could accept only the exchange of goods as the basis of their economic relationships with the socialist cities. Money was thus needed to regulate these exchanges, and communism could only come about when the two Soviet forms of property, the state and the cooperative, would merge into one single, moneyless national economic unit.

However, nothing prevented the state from "socializing" the collective farms as well, and thus from building a unitary system. Stalin, however, did not want to do it, possibly because War Communism and the 1929–30 crisis had taught him that without money, the Soviet system could not survive, even in the short term. He thus found justifications not to act (e.g., *kolkhoz* property was socialist property and therefore impossible to deal with as with capitalistic property) and reacted angrily to proposals to speed up the communist transformation of the countryside, such as those advanced by Khrushchev in early 1951.

The communist future thus became a mirage, and Stalin sensed there was no road that could lead to it. His solution was to reaffirm the validity of Marx's tenets, while at the same time proposing the postponement of the transition to communism by introducing yet new "stages" between the socialist and the communist ones, deferring the achievement of the latter to an ever remote future. The Soviet Union, Stalin explained, had entered a stage of preparation for the transition to communism, which meant building the "preliminary conditions for it": the old duo, "proletarian dictatorship-communism," became a trio in 1936 with the insertion of socialism (Graziosi, *L'Urss* 126 ff.), later to be expanded into a quartet.[8]

The fragile equilibrium of the mid-1930s started to break up in the face of pressure the state imposed upon the countryside in order to prepare for war, and then, and even more, to face the war's initial, terrible defeats. Threatened by Moscow, *kolkhoz* directors thought only about extracting the highest possible quantity of foodstuffs from their domains; at the same time goods disappeared from rural stores, and the police disbanded the queues of peasants that formed in front of stores in the cities. Before the war started, those who had not been able to flee the *kolkhozy* were often spending 70 percent of their time in the collective fields, often for little to no compensation (Graziosi, *L'Urss di Lenin* 463 ff.).

Between 1941 and 1945, starvation and suffering were universal and death, frequent. Nevertheless, crop yields, which were often lower than during the early 1930s, did not result in new mass famines. *Kolkhozniki* owed their survival to their private plots and to their cows. Yet the war and the pressure the state exerted upon the countryside struck another mortal blow to Soviet villages: after 1945, generally it was invalids who returned to them, strengthening the trend toward the aging and the feminization of their residents.

Above all, the war did not fully integrate peasants into the "Soviet *narod*." In the parts of the country that remained under Soviet control, it could have happened, and there certainly were steps in this direction. Stalin spoke to "brothers and sisters," Russian Orthodox churches were reopened and a patriarch re-elected, official propaganda rediscovered "national" traditions (and not only Russian ones)—and suffering could be justified by the need to vanquish foreign invaders.

Yet one must always remember that for some national groups the war meant a definite exclusion from that very *narod*, an exclusion for which they paid dearly (Polian). Ukraine came to occupy a sort of middle ground: its Western regions were considered de facto enemy territory, while its larger "Soviet" part was tarred by the undeserved sentence of "betrayal." This was seldom officially proclaimed but was in fact generally understood, although it should be remembered that in 1941 it was the Soviet Ukrainian Front that resisted longest and most valiantly. Above all, and more generally, once victory was achieved, the "pact" the villages were thought to have signed with the Soviet state did not materialize. NKVD-MVD reports from different

---

[8] Brezhnev later added one more stage to this scheme: "developed socialism."

regions tell us in detail, and with impressive uniformity, what the peasants were hoping for:

> Evdokiia Mikhailovna Bazhenova, from a kulak family (Rybnoe village), states: "Very soon collective farms will be disbanded. I just can't wait for it." Andrei Grigor'evich Samokhvalov, tractor brigadier from the Shumikhinskaya MTS, tells other tractor drivers: "Collective farms did not live up to expectations—that is why it's been decided to get rid of them"... Citizen Mariia Ignat'evna Mironova... declares that "England and America proposed that our government accept five conditions: to reintroduce epaulettes in the army, to open churches, to disband collective farms, to release all prisoners, and to send all the Jews to the front"... Citizen Agniia Filippovna Ozhgibesova declares: "Everybody is talking about it, soon there won't be collective farms anymore, churches will be reopened, and life will be good."... Collective farmer Anna Grigor'evna Porosenkova declares: "America gave Stalin three orders: reintroduce epaulettes in the army, open churches, and disband collective farms, then the war will end... we shall live as individual farmers. ("Iz ob"iasnitel'noi zapiski" 425–27)[9]

The post-war years brought instead a new famine (Zima), more work days *(trudodni)* in the collective farm fields, more work obligations *(trudpovinnosti)* of different sorts, more taxes in kind and financial on the LPKh, and more repression, especially after the passing of the cruel 1947 laws for the punishment of theft of private and state property, which ruined millions of lives and helped produce a new generation of people living a marginal existence *(marginaly)* (Krasil'nikov and Shadt; Kozlov; Zubkova and Zhukova). As General Vasilii Rybal'chenko told his colleague Fillip Gordov in December 1946, "We have adopted a policy such that nobody wants to work anymore. It must be openly said that all the *kolkhozniki* hate Stalin and wait for his death... They think that if Stalin dies, the *kolkhozy* will die too..." (Zubkova 155–56). Hundreds of interviews gathered after the war by the Harvard Project on the Soviet Social System fully confirm the

---

[9] Two years later, in 1945, peasants from different regions maintained, "During the San Francisco conference [establishing the United Nations], it was proposed to Molotov that the collective farms be disbanded, churches opened and free trade allowed."... As reported in one *kolkhoz*: "A special commission on dissolution of collective farms has been created in Moscow." Members of *kolkhoz* "Iskra" (in the Pskov region) ... asked one district worker: "How soon will collective farms be disbanded? If it was not for collective farms, we would live better and would bring more benefits to the state" (Livshin and Orlov 77–79).

point: hatred for Stalin and Communist Party leaders was higher among *kolkhozniki* than in any other social group.[10]

Meanwhile, an increase in economic and repressive pressure on both the *kolkhozy* and the LPKh was transforming the late Stalin countryside into a somber, darker replica of Mikhail Saltykov-Shchedrin's *Poshekhonskaia starina*. A self-pretending "modernity" had generated a quasi-servile system that was in many respects even harsher than, and of course quite different from, the *ancien régime*. After twenty-five years of pitiless exploitation, the Soviet countryside lay in ruin. Not surprisingly, when in the 1990s researchers tried to collect recollections from witnesses to events of the early 1930s, they met with peasants almost unable to make a distinction among the different parts of the 1929–1953 period. The whole era had solidified in their minds as one of state violence and intense suffering, of hunger and deprivation, thus making it difficult to use their testimonies.[11]

3. Soviet Leaders and the Peasant Tragedy

In spite of official pronouncements to the contrary, including their own, Stalin's top aides were fully aware of the Soviet agricultural disaster (Khlevniuk and Gorlizki 26–27, 186), as is clear from the measures they took to remedy the situation and to improve the lot of the collective farmer after the leader's death. One can therefore maintain that the most significant periods of Soviet reformism (1953–56) started as a reaction to the catastrophe that the years 1929–33 brought about in the countryside.[12]

What, then, was the post-Stalinist Soviet elite's relationship to, and awareness of, the peasants' misfortunes, the Holodomor, and the other famines of 1931–34? That elite's first generation had direct knowledge of these tragedies, which was refreshed by the 1946–47 famine, as is evident from the pages Khrushchev devotes in his memoirs to this topic (Khrushchev 9–17, 310–12). This knowledge, as well as the "common feeling" born out of the war and of victory, made Beria, Khrushchev,

---

[10] The rich Project materials are available at http://hcl.harvard.edu/collections/hpsss/about.html. Inkeles and Bauer provide a summation of the Project.

[11] This was also my experience when I briefly worked as a consultant for Serhiy Bukovsky's movie *Zhyvi / The Living*, which is based on some magnificent interviews. Albeit indirectly, Frank Sysyn raised a similar point in his "Ukrainian Famine," regarding the activities of the Ukrainian diaspora.

[12] This was not only a Soviet phenomenon: the Hungarian leader Imre Nagy directed a Siberian *kolkhoz* in the 1930s, and Czechoslovakian leader Alexander Dubček personally and deeply experienced the 1931–33 Kazakh horror as a child.

Malenkov and the Soviet top leadership not insensible to the plight of Ukraine and the collective farmers and created an atmosphere in which some pro-peasant measures were adopted in 1953-56.

Khrushchev's knowledge of Ukraine's repeated tragedies and the guilty feelings this knowledge generated are also evident in his ideas of a Ukraine so victimized as to deserve special compensation. On 20 June 1944, for instance, he wrote Stalin suggesting that Ukrainian territory be expanded westward to include what he deemed ethnically Russian and Ukrainian lands, Chełm (Ukrainian: Kholm) included. And a few months later he spoke for the first time of giving Crimea to Ukraine, from whence the Tatars had just been deported and therefore required resettlement: "Ukraine is in ruin, but everybody wants something from it. And what if we gave the Crimea to her, no strings attached?"[13] The poisonous "gift" of Crimea in 1954 thus might in some way be linked to an awareness that Ukraine somehow should be "repaid."[14] Brezhnev, too, who lived the first part of his life as a "Ukrainian" and only became a "Russian" later, had personal experience of the 1930s and shared similar feelings. Though he continued to vigorously enforce the famine taboo, he introduced in 1964-65 a minimal pension plan for *kolkhozniki,* and in 1974 he granted them the right to obtain internal passports, thus ending the most evident stigma of social inferiority that in 1932-33 had been imposed upon the countryside.

At the republican level, Ukrainian Party leader Petro Shelest, who had lived through collectivization and famine, went so far as to try to break the Holodomor taboo (Kul'chyts'ky 431-49). In 1967, after the first serious works on collectivization had been written, if not published, he demanded that the Party academic collective charged with writing a new history of socialist Ukraine add a paragraph on famine in 1932-33 to the chapter on collectivization. The group's members, quite embarrassed, did not dare do so, and Moscow's subsequent negative reactions to the idea proved their self-censorship prescient in its own way.

The taboo thus remained in force and was even reinforced in the 1970s and 1980s, in large measure as a reaction to advances in the knowledge of the Holodomor, owing to the efforts of the Ukrainian diaspora. One may surmise that the new generation of Soviet leaders that came to power in the

---

[13] Knyshevskii, P. "Strikhi k portretu kremlevskoi galerei." *Novoe vremia* 9 (1993). Cited in Shapoval, 29.

[14] All the same, the reality of the need for more effective administration of this economically depressed peninsula was the far more pertinent consideration in its transfer to the jurisdiction of the Ukrainian SSR. Sasse, Chapter Five, "Reassessing the 1954 Transfer of Crimea" 107-26.

1980s simply was unaware of the reality of the 1930s famines because of the taboo and their younger age and thus, lack of direct experience of earlier events. It follows that they were thus more open to discussing the matter as an issue that some really believed was being "distorted" by "capitalist propaganda." In a way, therefore, naïveté was a component (one among many) of what was to be famously termed glasnost.

The breaking of the Holodomor taboo was hastened by the spread of glasnost after the 1986 Chornobyl accident. Only twenty months later, at the end of 1987, Volodymyr Shcherbyts'kyi officially acknowledged that a famine had taken place in Ukraine in 1932–33. The process was perhaps also accelerated by the re-emergence of long-forgotten personal recollections among new leaders. As their own memoirs tell us, Gorbachev had lost three uncles to the famine in the North Caucasus and Yeltsin's family had been de-kulakized and deported: How could they have been indifferent to new stories about collectivization and hunger coming to the fore (Gorbachev; Yeltsin; Colton)?

This brings us again to the place that the Holodomor and the other famines of the early 1930s must be assigned in understanding the collapse of the USSR. The unquestionable early success of the 1953–56 agricultural reforms—which substantially increased the standard of living of the collective farm workers and the country as a whole, thereby partially altering the 1929–33 legacy—failed to spark a self-sustained development. This failure and the subsequent agricultural crisis provide us with yet another interesting perspective on this crucial event.

Those reforms represented a unique opportunity to reform the Soviet system and thus to secure its survival. Khrushchev (and Beriia and Malenkov before him) did much and found the courage to denounce Stalin, an unpopular move among Party cadres. But he left the essential structure of Stalin's system (quite unpopular among the *kolkhozniki*) substantially intact at a time in which the Soviet countryside still retained a certain amount of energy, and rural residents still represented more than 50 percent of the country's inhabitants. Khrushchev did this because he was personally convinced that the collectivized system built upon the great famines was indeed a superior one. In fact, in his "secret speech" he attacked Stalin for his cruelty, the great trials, and the Terror of the late 1930s as well as for the war's initial misfortunes, but passed very positive judgment upon his pre-1934 policies.

Only twenty years later, in 1976, China's Deng Xiaoping grappled with the legacy of the colossal famine caused by the Great Leap Forward (current estimates speak of 30 to 40 million victims). He had contributed to its unleashing but had quickly realized it was a tragic mistake. Relying on the policies devised in the first half of the 1960s to remedy that tragedy before

Mao initiated the catastrophic "Cultural Revolution," Deng dismantled Mao's system but preserved Mao's cult of personality in spite of his awareness of the man's responsibilities and crimes, which had personally affected him and his family.[15] Deng thus reversed the terms of Khrushchev's equation because he was convinced that the socialist economic system was doomed, especially in the countryside, and wanted to save the Chinese state and political system.

The initial success of the Soviet reforms during the 1950s and their subsequent failure are thus linked to the limited mental horizons of Khrushchev and the Soviet elites (with the possible exception of Beriia), which were largely determined by ideology. In other words, ideology and devotion to the past—rather than a lack of opportunity or courage—impeded a more profound transformation of the Soviet system in the crucial 1953 to 1964 decade, when a peasantry that could have profited from the disbanding of collective farms still existed. These conditions were absent thirty years later, when there were no peasants that could fuel a Gorbachev NEP, as they were doing for Deng. This difference should be sufficient enough to discount parallels between the two countries in the 1980s without even considering other major differences (e.g., the multinational and strategic position of the USSR).

4. Ukraine and the Holodomor: the National and Peasant Question in Soviet History

Intellectuals, in reaction to the peasants' fate, contributed to the great season of Soviet reforms: Tatiana Zaslavskaia and Iurii Arutiunian were, for example, shocked by the appalling poverty they encountered in the countryside while doing research for their doctorates (Zaslavskaya). Already in the early 1950s the village writers (mentioned earlier) were in fact dismantling the official version of collectivization. This "discovery" of rural misery followed different courses, but it was everywhere, Russia included, and was tied to a resurgence of national sentiment—often of the traditional pro-peasant variety.[16] Ukraine, where as we know the famine taboo was at its strongest, was the significant exception: here language was to serve as a catalyst for national revival.

---

[15] Regarding the situation in China, see Becker, Dikötter, Jisheng, Vogel, and Pantsov.
[16] After the publication of the first Russian edition of *The Great Soviet Peasant War*, I received an unexpected letter of support from Igor Shafarevich, who openly linked the destruction of the Russian nation conducted by communism to that of its peasantry.

I believe that this marked differentiation was linked in some manner to the extremely harsh lesson imparted to the Republic in 1930-34. After 1929, urban dwellers throughout the USSR, periodically screened and "cleansed," learned to shut their eyes before what happened in the countryside, which was soon isolated by a wall raised by the Holodomor and the other Soviet famines and then solidified by the servile system and new legal discriminations (the internal passport first of all) that defined it.

Urban inhabitants—many of whom had relatives in the villages and eyes to see—knew what was happening but presumably preferred not to, disassociating themselves from a world whose terrible desolation was best left not broached. To many, it must have seemed wiser to forget what happened there, under the protection afforded by the relatively generous, albeit in absolute terms miserable, privileges the regime granted to the urban population.

In Ukraine, the stigma was of a double nature: the December 1932 secret provisions on the reversal of Ukrainization (more on this later); the 1933 repression of those who had furthered the Republic's national-communist movement; and the policies directed at marginalizing and taming the Ukrainian language and so forth were reminders to all that it was more "convenient" to be an urban dweller and a Russified one.

Thus the wall separating the cities from the countryside in Ukraine grew thicker as a result of a dual process. Firstly, the regime's assault on the villages sent a clear signal to the large Russian and Jewish urban communities, which had often disliked, if not resented, Ukrainization, that things Ukrainian could now be discarded safely and that it was actually advisable to do so.[17] Secondly, the same signal sounded loudly and clearly for recently urbanized or newly arrived peasants of Ukrainian stock, who integrated themselves as quickly as possible into the revised urban norms in order to escape a fate that must have looked and indeed was terrible.

From 1933 onward, full urbanization *also* meant Russification, while Ukrainian was, at most, to be cherished as a folkloric remnant, tainted by its dangerous association with the village and its tragedies. The rediscovery of the Ukrainian language during the late 1950s was therefore, in a way, also an indirect rediscovery of the countryside and of its past, which could not be direct because of the strength of the Holodomor taboo and of the terrible lessons associated with it.

---

[17] Bulgakov's *The White Guard* provides one of the best depictions of the feelings of urban Russians, but one may find clear signs of similar sentiments in the policies followed by the 1919 Bolshevik Ukrainian government and in the 1925-27 polemics on the application of Ukrainization in the cities.

I mentioned the Jewish urban communities in association with the Russian ones. Yet this association is valid only in the case of the few, large cities and for the non-traditional minority of the Jewish world. The processes that devastated the ethnic Ukrainian communities in 1928–33 also badly damaged the majority of the Jewish-Ukrainian ones. Shtetls had been undermined already by the civil war and the great pogroms that accompanied it and were further drained of energy by the great migration of the 1920s to large Soviet Russian cities, something made possible by the abolition of discriminatory tsarist laws. Yet shtetls had largely survived, only to be hit in 1928 by the tightening persecution of their religious leaders and by the arrest and often the deportation of the shopkeepers, traders and merchants, small and medium industrialists, and artisans that marked the end of the NEP and the repression of the *nepmeny*. Soon afterwards, settlements that had thrived on a mutually beneficial albeit somewhat problematic association with Ukrainian villages were ruined by the desolation that de-kulakization, collectivization and eventually the Holodomor brought upon the latter. The devastation of rural Ukraine thus hit a plurality of the Republic's minority communities, the Mennonite included.

We thus come once more to the crucial issue of the linkage between the peasant and the national questions in Soviet history, a linkage essential to understanding the first decades of the Soviet Union including the role of the Holodomor and the other famines, the Kazakh first and foremost.[18] Both Lenin and Stalin understood this linkage very well.

"Land to the peasants" and the nation's "right of self-determination up to separation" were possibly the two most important innovations Lenin introduced in the Marxist vocabulary: the socialist "worker" revolution became possible precisely because he created the conditions for such a revolution to ride to power by surfing the interrelated peasant and national waves. And these waves were more powerful in places where the land was in "alien" hands, as was often the case in the empire's 'Ukraines,' where Polish, Russian and German lords, and Slavic colonists in Central Asia, controlled large swaths of territory.

Stalin theorized about the linkage between the peasant and the national question in his *Marxism and the National Question* (1913). In fact, the booklet's originality is rooted in the combination of Marxism, "evolutionism" and a Herderism that Stalin probably acquired via his

---

[18] Both Buttino and Pianciola, for example, have discussed convincingly the peculiar features the peasant/national connection took in "Russian" Turkestan and in Soviet Central Asia, where it was further complicated by religion.

previous contacts with the Georgian national movement and through his polemics with Otto Bauer and Austro-socialist nationality theory. Like Herder, Stalin saw in language the main—albeit not the sole—national marker, and he often reiterated Herder's basic tenet that each and every nationality possesses equal dignity. Stalin also accepted the concept of dominant and oppressed, or peasant, "peoples," and, like Bauer, supported the idea that the latter were not doomed to be absorbed by the former, as Marx and Engels had maintained in 1848. Rather, Stalin surmised that peasants—posited per Herder as the true repository of language and thus of the "*narod*"—could conquer "alien" cities and carry their nations to independence (Graziosi, *Vneshniaia i vnutrenniaia politika*; van Ree 41–65).

Nationalities, peasants and "peoples," or, more accurately, peasant peoples and peasant nations, thus became the revolution's most important "reserve." Initially, this was true for East Central Europe, but above all it included the European colonies, whose crucial role in the great world transformation of the twentieth century Lenin was perhaps the first to grasp fully. Both Lenin and Stalin thus came to see peasants as "material" that revolutionaries could manipulate in two ways: as the social explosive needed to unhinge the existing social and political order, and as a nation-building substance that had to be defused via industrialization and urbanization in order to deprive nationalism of its main spring and support.

The events of 1917 proved the first diagnosis right. Yet the experience of the civil war also taught Bolshevik leaders a different lesson. As Ukraine in 1919 or Western Siberia in 1920 (but also the Northern Caucasus and the Volga regions) indicated, precisely because they were a true revolutionary force, peasants were also extremely dangerous: like all volatile material, they could explode in the face of those trying to handle them. What is more, as in Ukraine during 1919, their upheavals could open the way to external enemies (this being perhaps Stalin's greatest fear in the early 1930s).

Peasants and peasant-nations were thus very useful, but they were also very dangerous.[19] In 1925, Stalin stated the link he established between the peasant and the national questions in crystal-clear terms:

> [T]he national question [is], in essence, a peasant question. Not an agrarian but a peasant question, for these are two different things. It is quite true

---

[19] The *Antonovshchina*, which as we know played a crucial role in Lenin's decision to abandon War Communism, fully confirmed the point. As Lenin himself was to state famously at the Tenth Party Congress, "This petty-bourgeois [i.e., peasant] counter-revolution is certainly more dangerous than Denikin, Yudenich and Kolchak combined."

that the national question must not be identified with the peasant question, for, in addition to peasant questions, the national question includes such questions as national culture, national statehood, etc. But it is also beyond doubt that, after all, the peasant question is the basis, the quintessence, of the national question. That explains the fact that the peasantry constitutes the main army of the national movement, that there is no powerful national movement without the peasant army, nor can there be. That is what is meant when it is said that, *in essence*, the national question is a peasant question. (*Bol'shevik* 7, 15 April 1925)[20]

In those very months, Marx's "primitive accumulation" theory, which Evgenii Preobrazhenskii and the Left applied to the Soviet case, fueled Stalin's views that would turn the countryside into the internal colonies, providing the means to solve the Soviet economic crisis and build socialism speedily. However, this required unleashing a full-scale attack against peasants and peasant-nations that had just proved their dangerousness. A new, harsh monarch, capable of winning this war, was thus needed. As Bukharin explained to Kamenev:

"Stalin's line (as expressed at the Plenum) is such: 1. Capitalism developed at the expense of the colonies, through loans, or through exploitation of workers. We don't have any colonies, they don't give us any loans, hence our basic resource is the tribute from the peasantry (You understand that this is the same as Preobrazhenskii's theory); 2. The more socialism grows, the more resistance it will encounter (see the phrase in the resolution)... This is idiotic illiteracy; 3. When tributes are required and resistance grows, you need strong leadership... Stalin reasons so: "I provided grain through extraordinary measures... If such measures are needed, I am the only one capable of enforcing them"... What is to be done? What do you do, when you deal with such an enemy: Genghis Khan — the low culture of the Central Committee... Stalin's policies are leading to a civil war. He will have to drown revolts in blood." (Fel'shtinskii 182-203; Graziosi, *Sovetskii soiuz*)

Being a war against the peasantry, the assault Stalin unleashed was also, according to his own theory, a war against peoples and nations in which the state could attempt to mold the countryside's "ethnographic material"[21] by resorting to repression, hunger, and language-cultural policies.

---

[20] Stalin added that without an understanding of this link, it would be impossible to grasp the profoundly popular and profoundly revolutionary character of the national movement.

[21] These are the words of a high-ranking OGPU official working in Ukraine in 1933 (Graziosi, *Lettere da Kharkov* 168).

As for Stalin himself, and thus also Stalinism, the strengthening of his personal dictatorship in 1929 was solidified and intensified by the "victory" over the peasants and peasant nations, Ukraine first of all. The fear of Stalin that dominated the country, from his closest collaborators to the lowliest *kolkhoznik*, played a crucial role in this process. What other feeling could one have for a man who, in order to hold on to power and solve the crisis the regime had fallen into as a consequence of his policies, had not hesitated to consign millions to die of hunger? The quality and the scale of this action went far beyond even the extremely low moral standard of Bolshevik leaders who readily shot tens of thousands of "enemies" at the start of collectivization but who were now overwhelmed—as the minutes of the Seventeenth Congress of the AUCP(B) in early 1934 reveal to those who read them attentively—by a catastrophe in which some saw the signs of their own impending doom.

Fear thus became a key building block of Stalin's cult. His internalization as an all-controlling, cruel father took a decisive step forward as a consequence of his brutal and massive use of hunger to "teach a lesson." After 1933, Stalin was no longer just a supreme leader; he became the father-owner (*padre-padrone*, as one would say in Italian), possessing the power of life and death over his subjects and the capability of exercising it without hesitation on an unprecedented scale, holding in his hands the fate of individuals as well as entire nationalities and social groups.

As Boris Pasternak so well understood (Pasternak 659), the famines marked a qualitative change in the lie that had grown with the Soviet regime since its inception, but with even greater speed after 1928. To suggest a brilliant future in which somebody could still believe in the face of a grim reality—as Gorky did with socialist realism—was very different from proclaiming that life had already become more joyful (even in the face of heaps of corpses) while asking to be thanked for it.

Those heaps of corpses of direct, innocent victims of state policy bring us to one of the most fundamental questions raised in Soviet history by the Holodomor and the other famines of 1931–33, not to mention other events such as the national deportations of 1943–44 that killed in a few months up to 20–25 percent of the "punished peoples" and the almost complete physical liquidation of the Orthodox Church in the 1930s. The question I am alluding to is, of course, genocide. Norman Naimark has recently and correctly reminded us of its crucial importance (Naimark; Kramer), stressing Stalin's personal role in Soviet genocides to which only his death put a sudden stop. A few years ago, in a personal letter to this writer, Oleg Khlevniuk pointed out that Stalin's mind usually worked along "genocidal" lines: "No matter what problem arose in the country, it was solved through the application of violence directed at specific and well-defined sociocultural or national groups of the population." These groups and their treatment varied over time, according to the internal and international situation, the despot's own beliefs, and the evolution of his paranoia, and thus of his cruelty.

In the case of the Holodomor, the trigger was Stalin's previously discussed combination of the social, i.e., the peasant, and the national factors. These pushed him in late fall 1932 to escalate what would have in due course become, by the spring of 1933, a serious but limited famine, caused by his own policies, into a Holodomor intended not to eradicate, but to emasculate the Ukrainian nation by breaking its peasantry and crippling its intellectual and political elite.[22] Once this is understood, the polemics between the "peasant" and the "national" interpretation of the Famine lose their raison d'être. Not surprisingly, as Terry Martin proved (Martin 273–308), Stalin was the first to give this famine a "national interpretation." Revealingly, the already mentioned secret 1932 decrees that reversed indigenization policies in Ukraine and in the Kuban were named "On Grain Procurements in Ukraine, the Northern Caucasus and the Western Oblast."[23] The decrees noted that those policies had not only failed to disarm nationalistic feelings in Ukraine but had even helped them grow, i.e., producing enemies with Party cards in their pockets. Peasants, therefore, were not the sole culprits of the crisis but shared responsibility with the Ukrainian cultural elites and the national-communist leadership.[24]

Ukrainization programs in the Russian republic were subsequently abolished, and several million Ukrainians living in the RSFSR lost the education, press, and self-government rights that other nationalities continued to enjoy. More important, an aggressive attack on the Ukrainian language was launched in Ukraine as well, contributing to the already mentioned re-Russification of the Ukrainian cities. Ukrainian again was to become a second-rate, subordinated language that people, intending to progress in life, had to abandon. Moreover, special policies were adopted to bring it normatively closer to Russian and to repress the thousands of cadres that had promoted it in previous years (Yefimenko 69-98). The Ukrainian peasants and intelligentsia and Ukrainian language and culture were thus subjected in 1932–34 to policies that, taken together, fully satisfy the definition of "genocide" as adopted by the United Nations.

---

[22] I elaborate on this point in *Soviet 1931–33 Famines* and in my forthcoming "The Uses of Hunger."

[23] For the text in English translation, see Klid and Motyl 245–47.

[24] In this and in the following paragraph, I follow my contribution "Stalin's Genocides, and…?"

This brings us for the last time to the role the Holodomor and the other famines of the early 1930s should play in attempts to assess the viability of the Soviet system and to understand the collapse of the USSR. What can it mean for a state and a regime to have a genocide (and in the Soviet case, possibly, more than one) lurking in its own past, and for a "system"—because the Soviet Union was indeed a particular social and economic system—to have been born out of a genocidal confrontation with the majority of its own population? More specifically, what consequences may have derived from concealing such a past under a heap of good words about that very system and its intentions, good words in which that very regime's elites at a certain point started to believe? What consequences did such a startling development of untruth have on Soviet history?

In such conditions, the understanding of the truth but also the simple intuition of it and its assertion, even and perhaps especially by former believers, may have an explosive impact, both at the personal and the social levels. In fact it did, and more than once, in Soviet history. The problem thus became how to avoid the resurfacing of truth. But over time, the growing ignorance of the past weakened the effort to control it. Above all, by their sheer "dimensions," the 1931–33 famines made it almost impossible to resolve the contradiction between official discourse and truth, thus laying the foundation for their recurrent exposition.

In this light, the Holodomor assumes the features of a formidable obstacle to the ability to reform a system that could not speak the truth about its own past and that was swept away when it came to light. Ironically, it was people who deemed the system's evolution possible and wanted to promote it by settling accounts with that past who often set this process in motion. What they discovered was that the legacy of the past could not be brought under their control, and its public exposure undermined the very legitimacy of the system they sincerely wished to amend.

Conclusions

I wish to conclude by examining the impact that the awareness of the Holodomor and the reality of rural life in the USSR in the 1930s may—or should—have on the image of the Soviet Union during that decade and therefore also on the various images produced over time by students and observers of the Soviet system.

Soviet historians in the West have often been divided into two opposing groups, the so-called totalitarian school and the anti-totalitarian (revisionist) one, which included the social historians of the 1970s and 1980s. It is my impression that the Holodomor, the Kazakh famine, the brutality of de-kulakization and collectivization, the unquestionable mass peasant opposition to the regime (with peasants, including nomads, making up nearly 80 percent of the Soviet population), and the chaos, suffering, and misery that dominated rural life for years, belie any interpretations of Stalin's USSR as a modern system that had the support of a substantial part of the population whose conscience it successfully manipulated.

What we have learned since 1991 about the repressions of 1937-38—a series of pre-emptive, mass cleansing operations rather than a random resort to terror in order to "atomize" the population—also seems to confirm the need for a new image of the USSR in the 1930s. Those very "mass operations" also confirm the weak legitimacy as well as the profound unpopularity of a regime that in peacetime deemed necessary to execute in sixteen months some 700,000 internal enemies, a rather unique case in history.

In fact, the Stalinist regime resembles much more an "evil empire" built upon the oppression of villages and peoples (but also of workers and intellectuals) than a modern "totalitarianism" capable of controlling and mobilizing its "citizens." This does not deny that the Stalinist system also had, and built, its own supporting groups and strata as well as the obvious fact that there also was a Soviet "modernization," with its accompanying urbanization, industrialization, and the like, which indeed ended up producing a Soviet "modernity."

Yet, both the totalitarian and the revisionist schools may have given too much credit to a Soviet "modernity," even if from radically divergent approaches. In the 1930s Soviet modernity was still little more than a project whose realization went hand in hand with the reproduction of elements and institutions that can only be defined in terms of a "return to a (non-existent) past": agrarian servitude, mass famines, cannibalism, primitive varieties of forced labour, the destruction of trade unions and of social welfare provisions, systematic torture, witch hunts, and the like.

Even later, Soviet modernity was a system in which status and personal connections (*sviazy*) were more important than money, as was typical of traditional societies. Moreover, it was dominated by an extremely statist, isolationist, and authoritarian regime, in which political power was thoroughly intertwined with an official, para-religious ideology. Resorting to an oxymoron, the postwar USSR could thus be termed a "modern" *ancien régime*, and in the long run it also could not survive because of this contradictory nature. For this very reason, I deem it untenable to analyze the course of its life just in terms of "modernization."[25]

There had been after the Second World War, and especially after 1953, a Soviet modernity, and one may perhaps speak of a Soviet "totalitarianism" of the Brezhnev years, a totalitarianism built upon a cocktail of control, modernity, fear, welfare, and victory-related legitimacy, but definitely not the mass violence and repression of the Stalin era.

Before 1941, however, the clash between the state, the peasantry and the nationalities—and we know how much and how closely these two "questions" were related, and not only in Stalin's mind—occupied centre stage. It seems to me that both the totalitarian and the anti-totalitarian schools missed this crucial point, and thus in a way fell victim to the taboo on peasants and nationalities that Stalin built around Soviet history, a taboo of which the Holodomor was for decades the lynchpin.

WORKS CITED

Becker, Jasper. *Hungry Ghosts: Mao's Secret Famine.* New York: The Free Press, 1996. Print.

Beznin, Mikhail and Tat'iana Dimoni. "Povinnosti rossiiskikh kolkhoznikov v 1930-1960-e gody." *Otechestvennaia istoriia* 2 (2002): 96-111. Print.

Beznin, Mikhail, Tat'iana Dimoni, and Larisa Iziumova. *Povinnosti rossiiskogo krest'ianstva v 1930-1960-kh godakh.* Vologda: Vologodskii NKTS TSĖMI RAN, 2001. Print.

Buttino, Marko. Revoliutsiia naoborot. Sredniaia Aziia mezhdu padeniem tsarskoi imperii i obrazovaniem SSSR. Moscow: Zven'ia, 2007. Print.

Chernyaev, Anatoly. *My Six Years with Gorbachev.* University Park: Pennsylvania State University Press, 2000. Print.

Colton, Timothy. *Yeltsin: A Life.* New York: Basic Books, 2008. Print.

Danilov, Viktor, Roberta Manning, and Lynne Viola, eds. Tragediia sovetskoi derevni: Kollektivizatsiia i raskulachivanie: Dokumenty i materialy v 5 tomakh, 1927-1939. 5 vols. Moscow: Rosspen, 1999-2006. Print.

Devis, Robert and Oleg Khlevniuk. "Otmena kartochnoi sistemy v SSSR. 1934-1935 gody." *Otechestvennaia istoriia* 5 (1999): 87-108. Print.

Dikötter, Frank. Mao's Great Famine: The History of China's Most Devastating Catastrophe, 1958-1962. New York: Walker & Co., 2010. Print.

Fel'shtinskii, Iurii. "Dva epizoda iz istorii vnutripartiinnoi bor'by: konfidenstial'nye besedy Bukharina." *Voprosy istorii* 2-3 (1991): 182-203. Print.

Fitzpatrick, Sheila. Stalin's Peasants: Resistance and Survival in the Russian Village After Collectivization. New York: Oxford University Press, 1994. Print.

---

[25] More on the question of Soviet "modernity" and on the debate between the "modernist" and the "neo-traditionalist" interpretation of the Soviet experiment can be found in *Qu'est-ce que l'Union soviétique? Intérpretations, historiographies, mythologies* (Graziosi, *Histoire de l'URSS* 359–84).

Gorbachev, Mikhail. *Memoirs*. New York: Doubleday, 1996. Print.
---. *Naedine s soboi*. Moscow: Grin Strit, 2012. Print.
Graziosi, Andrea. *The Great Soviet Peasant War. Bolsheviks and Peasants, 1918-1934*. Cambridge, MA: Harvard Ukrainian Research Institute, 1996. Print.
---. *Histoire de l'URSS*. Paris: PUF, 2010. Print.
---. "The Great Famine of 1932-33: Consequences and Implications." *Harvard Ukrainian Studies* 25.3-4 (2001): 157-166. Print.
---. L'Urss dal trionfo al degrado. Storia dell'Unione sovietica, 1945-1991. Bologna: Il Mulino, 2008. Print.
---. L'Urss di Lenin e Stalin. Storia dell'Unione sovietica, 1914-1945. Bologna: Il Mulino, 2007. Print.
---. *Lettere da Kharkov*. Turin: Einaudi, 1991. Print.
---. Sovetskii soiuz v 209 tsitatakh, 1914-1991. Moscow: Rosspen, 2010. Print.
---. "The Soviet 1931-33 Famines and the Ukrainian Holodomor: Is a New Interpretation Possible, What Would Its Consequences Be?" *Hunger by Design: The Great Ukrainian Famine and Its Soviet Context*. Ed. Halyna Hryn. Cambridge, MA: Harvard University Press, 2009. 1-19. Print.
---. "Stalin, krest'ianstvo i gosudarstvennyi socializm: evoliutsiia vzaimootnoshenii, 1927-1951 gg." *Istoriia Stalinizma: krest'iastvo i vlast'*. Moscow: Rosspen, 2011. 12-32. Print.
---. "Stalin's Genocides, and...?", Forum: Reappraising Mass Terror, Repression, and Responsibility in Stalin's Regime, Perspectives on Norman Naimark's Stalin's Genocides. *Journal of Cold War Studies* 14.3 (2012): 155-69. Print.
---. "The Uses of Hunger: Stalin's Solution and the Peasant and National Questions in Soviet Ukraine, 1932-1933." *Famines in European Economic History: The Last Great European Famines Reconsidered*. Ed. D. Curran, L. Luciuk and A. Newby. London and New-York: Routledge, forthcoming. Print.
---. "Vneshniaia i vnutrennaia politika Stalina: o natsional'nom voprose v imperskom kontekste, 1901-1926 gg." *Istoriia Stalinizma: itogi i problemy izucheniia*. Ed. Joerg Baberowski et al. Moscow: Rosspen, 2011. 215-35. Print.
Hessler, Julie. A Social History of Soviet Trade: Trade Policy, Retail Practices, and Consumption, 1917-1953. Princeton: Princeton University Press, 2004. Print.
Inkeles, Alex and Raymond A. Bauer, *The Soviet Citizen: Daily Life in a Totalitarian Society*. Cambridge, MA: Harvard University Press, 1959. Print.
"Iz ob"iasnitel'noi zapiski v sel'skokhoziaistvennyi otdel TsK VKP(b) o priusadebnykh uchastkakh kolkhoznikov Sverdlovskoi oblasti, mai 1939 g." *Kolkhoznaia zhizn' na Urale*. Ed. Jan Kessler and G. Kornilov. 111-15. Print.
Jisheng, Yang. *Tombstone. The Great Chinese Famine, 1958-1962*. New York: Farrar, Straus and Giroux, 2012. Print.
Kessler, Jan and G. Kornilov, eds. *Kolkhoznaia zhizn' na Urale, 1935-1953*. Moscow: Rosspen, 2006. Print.
Khlevniuk, Oleg et al., eds. *Pis'ma I.V. Stalina V.M. Molotovu 1925-1936 gg*. Moscow: Rossiia Molodaia, 1995. Print.
Khlevniuk, Oleg and Yoram Gorlizki. *Cold Peace: Stalin and the Soviet Ruling Circle, 1945-53*. Oxford: Oxford Unversity Press, 2004. Print.
Khrushchev, Nikita. *Memoirs of Nikita Khrushchev*, vol 2: *Reformer [1945-1964]*. Ed. Sergei Khrushchev. University Park, PA: Pennsylvania State University, 2006. Print.

Klid, Bohdan and Alexander J. Motyl, eds. *The Holodomor Reader: A Sourcebook on the Famine of 1932-1933 in Ukraine*. Edmonton and Toronto: Canadian Institute of Ukrainian Studies Press, 2012. Print.
Kozlov, Vladimir. Massovye besporiadki v SSSR pri Khrushcheve i Brezhneve, 1953-nachalo 1980-kh gg. Novosibirsk: Sibirskii khronograf, 1999. Print.
Kramer, Mark, ed. "Perspectives on Norman Naimark's Stalin's Genocides." *Journal of Cold War Studies* 14.3 (2012): 149-89. Print.
Krasil'nikov, Sergei and Aleksandr Shadt, eds., *Marginaly v sovetskom sotsiume, 1930-e - seredina 1950-kh gg*. Novosibirsk: RAN NGU, 2010. Print.
Krasil'nikov, Sergei. "Repressivnoe raskrest'ianivanie v 1930-e gody." *Istoriia Stalinizma: krest'ianstvo i vlast'*. Moscow: Rosspen, 2011. 45-55. Print.
Kul'chyts'ky, Stanislav. "Il tema della carestia nella vita politica e sociale dell'Ucraina alla fine degli anni Ottanta." *La morte della terra. La grande carestia in Ucraina nel 1932-33*. Ed. G. De Rosa and F. Lomastro. Rome: Viella, 2004. 431-49. Print.
Lewin, Moshe. The Making of the Soviet System: Essays in the Social History of Interwar Russia. New York: The New Press, 1985. Print.
Lih, Lars T., Oleg V. Naumov, and Oleg T. Khlevniuk. *Stalin's Letters to Molotov, 1925-1936*. New Haven and London: Yale University Press, 1995. Print.
Livshin, A.I and I.B. Orlov, eds. *Sovetskaia povsednevnost' i massovoe soznanie. 1939-1945*. Moscow: Rosspen, 2003. Print.
Maksudov, Sergei. "Dehumanization: The Change in the Moral and Ethical Consciousness of Soviet Citizens as a Result of Collectivization and Famine." *After the Holodomor: The Enduring Impact of the Great Famine on Ukraine*. Ed. Andrea Graziosi, Lubomyr Hajda and Halyna Hryn. Cambridge, MA: Harvard Ukrainian Research Institute, 2013. 123-48. Print.
Martin, Terry. *The Affirmative Action Empire: Nations and Nationalism in the Soviet Union, 1923-1939*. Ithaca, NY: Cornell University Press, 2001. Print.
Meslé, France and Jacques Vallin, *Mortalité et causes de décès en Ukraine aux XXe siècle*. Paris: Institut national d'études démographiques, 2003. Print.
Naimark, Norman. *Stalin's Genocides*. Princeton, N.J.: Princeton University Press, 2010. Print.
Pantsov, Alexander. *Mao: The Real Story*. New York: Simon & Schuster, 2012. Print.
Pasternak, Boris. *Il dottor Živago*. Milano: Feltrinelli, 1957. Print.
Pianciola, Nicola. Stalinismo di frontiera. Colonizzazione agricola, sterminio dei nomadi e costruzione statale in Asia centrale (1905-1936). Roma: Viella, 2009. Print.
"Pis'mo iz kolkhoza "1-e Maia" Uinskogo raiona Sverdlovskoi oblasti, 18 ianvaria 1938 g." *Kolkhoznaia zhizn' na Urale, 1935-1953*. Ed. Jan Kessler and G. Kornilov. Moscow: Rosspen, 2006. 134-41. Print.
Polian, Pavel. Ne po svoei vole: istoriia i geografiia prinuditel'nykh migratsii v SSSR. Moscow: Memorial, 2001. Print.
Popov, Vasilii, ed. *Rossiiskaia derevnia posle voiny, 1945-1953*, Moscow: Prometei, 1993. Print.
Sasse, Gwendolyn. *The Crimea Question: Identity, Transition, and Conflict*. Cambridge, MA: Harvard Ukrainian Research Institute, 2007. Print.
Shapoval, Iurii. "The Ukrainian Years, 1894-1949." *Nikita Khrushchev*. Ed. William Taubman, Sergei Khrushchev, and Abbott Gleason. New Haven: Yale University Press, 2000. 8-43. Print.

Stalin, Iosif. "Iz rechi v komissii 2-go Vsesoiuznogo s"ezda kolkhoznikov udarnikov." *Pravda*, 15 March 1935. Print.

Stalin, Iosif. *Ekonomicheskie problemy sotsializma v SSSR*. Moscow: Gos. Izd-vo polit. lit-ry, 1952. Print.

Sysyn, Frank. "The Ukrainian Famine of 1932-33: The Role of the Ukrainian Diaspora in Research and Public Discussion." *Studies in Comparative Genocides*. Ed. Levon Chorbajian and and George Shirinian. New York: St. Martin's Press, 1999. 182-215. Print.

van Ree, Erik. The Political Thought of Joseph Stalin: A Study in Twentieth-Century Revolutionary Patriotism. London: Routledge, 2002. Print.

---. "Heroes and Merchants: Stalin's Understanding of National Character." *Kritika: Explorations in Russian and Eurasian History* 1 (2007): 41-65. Print.

Vogel, Ezra. *Deng Xiaoping and the Transformation of China*. Cambridge, MA: Harvard University Press, 2011. Print.

Werth, Nicholas and Alex Berelowitch, eds. L'Etat soviétique contre les paysans. Rapports secrets de la police politique. Paris: Tallandier, 2011. Print.

Yefimenko, Hennadii. "The Kremlin's Nationality Policy in Ukraine after the Holodomor of 1932-33." *After the Holodomor: The Enduring Impact of the Great Famine on Ukraine*. Ed. Andrea Graziosi et al. Cambridge, MA: Harvard Ukrainian Research Institute, 2014. 69-98. Print.

Yeltsin, Boris. *Against the Grain: An Autobiography*. New York: Summit Books, 1990. Print.

Zaslavskaya, Tatyana. *The Second Socialist Revolution*. London: Tauris, 1990. Print.

Zima, Veniamin. Golod v SSSR. 1946-1947 godov: proiskhodzhenie i posledstviia. Moscow: IRI RAN, 1996. Print.

Zubkova, Elena. Poslevoennoe sovetskoe obshchestvo. Politika i povsednevnost', 1945-1953. Moscow: Rosspen, 2000. Print.

Zubkova, Elena and T. Iu. Zhukova, eds. Na "kraiu" sovestkogo obshchestva. Sotsial'nye marginaly kak ob"ekt gosudarstvennoi politiki, 1945-1960-e gg. Moscow: Rosspen, 2010. Print

Reflections on Stalin and the Holodomor

Françoise Thom
Paris-Sorbonne University (Paris IV)

Abstract: The mechanisms and the chronology of the great crimes committed by totalitarian regimes are now well documented. While they may explain the mechanics of these events, they do not always explain *why* they transpired. The implementation of Stalin's policy of collectivization and de-kulakization relied on dissimulation. Moreover, the pace of collectivization was justified by external threats, initially from Great Britain and Poland, and later extending to Japan. This made possible the branding of any political adversary as a traitor. As long as Stalin faced organized political opposition, he was unable to launch any maximal policies. After the defeat of Trotsky in December 1927 he was able to create crisis situations that ultimately furthered his own power. The offensive he unleashed against the peasants became a means of reinforcing his increasing dictatorship. The collectivization campaign employed the rational argument that the backward countryside needed to modernize production. Its ultimate aim, however, was the crushing of an independent peasantry. There are enlightening comparisons that can be made between collectivization in China and the USSR, which are explored in this essay. The resistance to collectivization was particularly strong amongst Ukrainians. Stalin, who had long regarded the national question as inseparable from the peasant question, deliberately chose mass starvation to break resistance to his will. The history of these events was for a long time shrouded in great secrecy until it began being discussed by Western scholars, becoming a matter of considerable debate between the "totalitarian" and "revisionist" schools of Soviet historiography.

Keywords: Holodomor, Collectivization, China, USSR, Peasantry, Starvation

> "Devastation as a principle of government!
> This is unprecedented in history..."
> P. A. Valuev (1865)[1]

The mechanisms and the chronological sequence of the great crimes committed by totalitarian regimes are now well documented. But this does not mean that the mystery of those moments of criminal folly engulfing a whole society is solved. We see links in the chain of events, we know by what arguments decisions were rationalized, and we can name

---

[1] Qtd. in Getmanskii 43.

those responsible for the crimes. But ultimately a question remains: how can one explain that the instinct of self-preservation of a whole society has been disconnected, that plain common sense seems to have deserted the ruling group and those who are ruled, that elementary moral principles cease to exist? How can a leader impose a spiral of destruction and terror on his often-reluctant followers? Why does the ruling group accept its part in implementing policies whose disastrous consequences it understands? These questions apply to the Soviet Union under Stalin as well as Nazi Germany or Maoist China.

First we will try to understand *how* Stalin imposed the policy of collectivization and de-kulakization on the Politburo and the Communist apparatus. His tactics relied on dissimulation. For many Communists, Lenin's New Economic Policy (NEP) had been a forced and temporary compromise with the peasant masses. But the relative economic independence of the peasants was considered a potential threat to the survival of the Bolshevik regime. Apparently Stalin easily could have persuaded his colleagues that Bolshevik rule should be imposed on the peasants as it was on the rest of Soviet society. Nevertheless he chose to take his Politburo colleagues by surprise by hiding his designs until the last minute. In 1926, when he was still in need of "rightists" to defeat the Trotskyists, he criticized Evgenii Preobrazhenskii for advocating a policy towards the Soviet peasantry that was equivalent to the exploitation of the colonies by capitalist countries and for wanting to ensure "primitive socialist accumulation" at the expense of peasants (Souvarine 364). On 16 February 1928, he wrote in *Pravda*: "The kulak was enriched more than others..." To this he added, "The NEP is the foundation of our economy and will remain so for a long time." At the July 1928 Plenum of the All-Union Communist Party (Bolshevik) (AUCP[B]), he proclaimed: "Our policy is not to stir up the class struggle... We have no interest in the class struggle taking the form of a civil war." Stalin had so well hidden his intentions that in early September 1929, Grigorii Ordzhonikidze, one of his closest associates, still maintained that total collectivization would take "years and years" (Conquest 118).

The ruthless pace of collectivization would have been difficult to justify had Stalin had not whipped up a huge war scare: Tense relations with Great Britain after the breaking off of diplomatic relations following the Arcos Affair in May 1927, and the murder of Petr Voikov, the Soviet representative in Poland, heralded by the Kremlin as a new Sarajevo, furnished Stalin a pretext to depict the USSR as a country surrounded by enemies intent on unleashing war on the socialist fatherland. This, in turn, allowed any political adversary to be branded as a traitor. Already in April 1927 at the Sixteenth Party Conference, Stalin tests the waters in this regard, stating, "It is impossible to develop a real struggle against class enemies if we have their agents in our ranks." Dissidents are labelled as traitors. This background of hysterical paranoia is one of the factors explaining the paralysis of society in advance of the total offensive of the Stalinist group.

In December 1927, Leon Trotsky and Grigorii Zinov'ev are expelled from the Politburo. As long as an organized opposition existed in the USSR, Stalin could not launch potentially disastrous policies because his adversaries could use fiascos against him. After the defeat of Trotsky and his allies, Stalin knew he could take risks. In January 1928, the first "extraordinary measures" against the peasants were adopted. Already in the summer of 1928 the catastrophic consequences of this policy were obvious. Stalin does not back down. In fact, he resumes political manoeuvres. Whether against individuals or groups, Stalin's offensives are always gradual, sometimes spread over a very long time. A wave is followed by a retreat and then a new wave that goes further. There is a kind of inexorable crescendo that culminates with Stalin's victory. After the first offensive against the "rightists" in the spring of 1928, when "extraordinary measures" led to shortages and a powerful wave of discontent in the country, Stalin is forced to retreat. At the Plenum of 4–12 July 1928, he pretends to take into account the arguments of the "rightists." He announces that "extraordinary measures" are temporarily suspended and stresses that those who want to implement them on a permanent basis are wrong (Stalin, "Ob industrializatsii"). Of course, all these concessions were ephemeral and Stalin soon resumed the offensive. In the spring of 1929 the "rightists" were routed. The same scenario of temporary concessions and further radicalization was repeated in 1930 and the following years.

In February–May 1930, Ukraine and Belarus were shaken by peasant revolts in reaction to collectivization, so that at the beginning of 1930 the Soviet leaders feared that peasants would refuse to sow. At the same time Stalin was worried about the possibility of a joint invasion of the Soviet Union by Poland and Japan (Ken and Rupasov 71). For those reasons he pretended to offer a truce to the peasants in March, when he wrote his famous article "Dizzy with Success" (March 2) and momentarily suspended collectivization. This blowing hot and cold, this alternation of hope and certainty of the worst, of radical ultra-leftist policies and unexpected limited relaxation, this succession of "abuses" and the denouncing of "abuses" with exemplary punishment of the culprits, explains why resistance fails to crystallize. The French historian Alphonse Aulard wrote about Robespierre: "He weighs on minds like the tyranny of uncertainty" (Furet and Ozouf 257). This fully applies to Stalin as well.

From this time forward, as in the early years of Bolshevik rule, any setback is used as a pretext for tightening the screws. The crisis unleashed by the offensive against the peasants becomes a means of reinforcing a dictatorship. Chronic crisis and selective starvation become the way to absolute power. The appalling consequences of earlier measures lead to the adoption of even worse, more radical policies. Combined with hysterical propaganda about the threat of foreign intervention, the critical situation provides a pretext to silence the opposition. Thus, the severity of the crisis unleashed by Stalin, far from diminishing his power, strengthens his position. The horrendous situation gives him a way to blackmail possible opponents: Who if not a traitor would cause a split when the country is on the brink of an abyss? Nikolai Bukharin's case illustrates the success of this tactic. In August 1928 he wrote to Stalin: "I already told you I will not fight you and I do not want to fight. I know only too well what a fight can cost, especially in the serious situation in which the country and the Party find themselves" (Kvashonkin 40). In his speech to the Politburo on 30 January 1929 Bukharin does not mince words in criticizing the peasant policy of Stalin, but he concludes with these words: "The challenges the country faces are so immense that it would be a truly criminal loss of strength and time to unleash a fight at the top" (Danilov vol. 1, 528)—before asking to be released from his duties.

It should also be noted that Stalin took great care not to confront all social groups at the same time. As in foreign policy, his purpose was always to avoid any building-up of a united front against him. Thus, in June 1931, when he was planning to inflict the coup de grâce to the peasantry, Stalin ended the process initiated in 1928 by the Shakhty trial that sparked the hunt for "bourgeois specialists." He suddenly discovered that the harassment of experts and egalitarianism was harmful, that an engineer of the old school was not necessarily a saboteur.

Finally we should take into account Stalin's colossal hypocrisy, a permanent feature of totalitarian regimes. Collectivization was first trumpeted by propaganda as a policy of "social justice" in favor of the poor peasants. It is only in 1932 that Stalin drops the mask, and it becomes clear that the Party has unleashed total war against the peasantry as a whole. In his memoirs Kandid Charkviani, who served as first secretary of Georgia from 1938 to 1952, gives us a striking example of Stalin's hypocrisy.

> In 1931 Stalin was on vacation in Georgia. He summoned the leader of the Georgian Communist Party, Samson Mamulia, and the Prime Minister Lado (aka Levan) Sukhishvili. Stalin asked Mamulia: "How are the collective farms?" "The situation is bad, Comrade Stalin," replied Mamulia. "Some kolkhozes are unraveling. We have to arm the Communists to neutralize

hostile elements and keep the peasants in collective farms." Stalin exploded: "You claim that the peasants should be herded into collective farms by the force of arms! What about voluntary adhesion to the *kolkhoz*, what about the interests of poor and middle peasants???" (Charkviani 452)

Thus, Stalin turned against the very people who had applied his policy, playing the role of the righter of wrongs.

This mad and criminal policy is camouflaged by seemingly rational arguments. Collectivization is justified by the need to urbanize the backward countryside, to modernize production. Stalin is fighting against barbarism by barbaric but necessary methods. He wants "giant collective farms" through which Soviet agriculture will have a rational, scientific basis. The tractor will displace the horse, and an army of agronomists will stimulate the development of production based on collective effort. This technocratic propaganda will even be accepted and spread by some foreign observers eager to minimize the horrors of de-kulakization and to find excuses for Stalin.

As a matter of fact, Stalin was pursuing rational aims through this policy: He was reinforcing his power. In launching collectivization, Stalin intended to crush not only the peasantry. He had also begun the process, which was to be completed in 1938-39, of the liquidation of the old Bolshevik guard and the radical renewal of the Party from the bottom up. At the Plenum of July 1928 (mentioned above), Stalin voiced his belief that the current difficulties would result ultimately in a strengthening of the Bolshevik ranks. Forcing the local Bolshevik leaders to implement collectivization was a sure means to discredit and destroy them in the eyes of the people: thus it was the first step of Stalin's policy of eliminating the older generation of Bolsheviks and replacing them with young careerists devoted to him. The example of collectivization in Transcaucasia is significant from this point of view. Stalin used collectivization as a pretext to begin the dismantlement of the Ordzhonikidze clan. From 1929 on, Beria, then chief of the Georgian GPU, wrote scathing reports on the disasters caused by this policy, laying the blame on the leading Communists Lela Kartvelishvili or Mamulia, protégés of Ordzhonikidze. Thus in March 1929, after the crushing of an uprising in Adzharia, Beria wrote: "Now that the attempt to revolt is liquidated, we have to analyze its causes. For us there is no doubt that they are to be found in certain measures adopted by the Party organizations and the organizations of Soviets, which are isolated from the masses and do not take into account their state of mind..." (cited in Sokolov 40-47). Stalin was so enchanted by Beria's competent denouncing of the Transcaucasian Bolsheviks that he promoted him to head of the Georgian Party in 1931 and of the Party in Transcaucasia in 1932, destroying

Ordzhonikidze's regional power base (Thom 27–35). He was so pleased with Beria that he accepted the lowering of the grain requirements for Beria's fiefdom.

Another obvious illustration of this strategy is the replacement of the "rightist" Aleksei Rykov as the head of the government by the reliable Viacheslav Molotov, signifying the takeover of the government by the Stalinist faction. On 13 September 1930, Stalin wrote to Molotov: "The council of the deputies of the Chairman of *Sovnarkom* has a tendency to become the headquarters of the opposition to the Central Committee" (Khlevniuk, Forgues and Werth 52). The solution was to appoint the loyal Molotov as chairman of the *Sovnarkom*. On December 19, Rykov was fired: "We finally have perfect unity at the top of the state and Party, which will strengthen our power." "The leaders of the Party and the Soviet apparatus will form a single fist," said the head of the Communist Party (Bolshevik) of Ukraine, Stanislav Kosior, who took the formal initiative of proposing this measure (Danilov vol. 2, 772). In late December the merger of state and Party at the highest level was accomplished.

Throughout his war against the peasantry, Stalin will make successive purges in the Party, removing, layer by layer and at all levels, those who are suspected of pity for the kulak, those who had floundered. This very special selection will create a party formed by ruthless individuals desperate to please the Leader. This aspect of collectivization as a "pedagogy" for the Party is clear in a speech by Molotov on 18 March 1930, in which he accused the local Party authorities of not having taken a sufficiently active role in de-kulakization, preferring to rely on the OGPU.

A comparison between collectivization in China and the USSR is enlightening. The Communist systems relied on total destruction of political institutions. For this reason, having reached the top of the Party apparatus, the ruling despot has only to fear the Communist establishment, the sole limit on his power. The history of both Stalin's and Mao's reigns can be interpreted as the history of their struggles against the Party establishment. In the early 1950s Mao wanted to abandon the policy of "new democracy," which allowed the Communists to take power on a relatively moderate program and to begin immediately the transition towards "socialism." Mao's closest colleagues, such as Liu Shaoqi, were opposed to this new orientation. Mao imposed his views in the summer of 1953, but already in 1955 the disastrous effects of Mao's first collectivization were obvious. In the spring of 1956 Liu and Zhou Enlai concluded an alliance and forced Mao to stop hasty collectivization. This resistance of top Party leaders and the solidarity they had displayed among themselves infuriated Mao. He chose extreme radicalization to defeat them: In 1957–58 he launched the Great Leap Forward, which resulted in 35 million deaths. The campaign for the establishment of "people's communes" was unleashed at the same time Mao provoked huge international tensions by bombing the Taiwanese islands of Quemoy and Matsu in August 1958. The ensuing disaster lead to a reaction by the Party establishment: In January 1962 Mao's policy is criticised by his close associates, Liu, Zhou and Deng Xiaoping. Mao is sidelined in the Party leadership. In response, Mao decides to destroy the existing Party and to replace it from top to bottom. He builds his faction with the support of the security apparatus and the military, controlled by Lin Biao (then his closest associate), and launches the Cultural Revolution in 1966, which leads China to anarchy and civil war. Thus Mao turned to extreme radicalism to defeat his colleagues (this is the central premise of Domenach).

The analogy with Stalin's tactic is obvious. As I have shown, Stalin's aim was to use collectivization to proceed to his own revolution and to get rid of the old Bolshevik guard; as in China's case, revolutionary maximalism was a weapon aimed at the Party establishment. Unlike Mao's, Stalin's power was apparently unscathed after the tragedy of collectivization. Nevertheless, historians have rightly pointed out that the great purges of 1937–38 were an aftermath of collectivization. The trauma left by this experience in the Party was deep: the mysterious Kremlin affair in 1935 that led to the demise of the Old Bolshevik Avel Enukidze and prepared the ground for the later purges reflects the turmoil in the higher circles of the Kremlin. Like Mao, Stalin decided to build a new Party in 1936–37. During the great purges, there were frequent accusations that a person disapproved of collectivization. In his famous speech at the Military Council on 2 June 1937, Stalin heaped scorn on Enukidze: "Can you imagine, this bastard Enukidze felt pity for the peasants. And since he can play the simpleton, this beanpole, people believed him…" (Stalin 214–35). After his arrest, Mikhail Frinovskii, Ezhov's deputy, confessed that Efim Evdokimov, the former chief of the secret operational department of the OGPU, told him at the time that he thought the liquidation of kulaks was wrong and that he did not believe in the success of this policy, convinced that it would ruin the villages and destroy agriculture (Khaustov et al 35). And again, in 1952, a few months before his death, Stalin adopted an ultra-leftist program as preparation for the elimination of the main group of the Politburo. Ultimately, both Stalin and Mao failed to defeat the Party establishment because by extreme policies they undermined their own factions.

For Stalin, reinforcing his personal power and reinforcing the power of the Soviet state amounted to one and the same thing. Here we find his second goal for launching collectivization and organizing famine in Ukraine. In 1928, Stalin decides to transform the Soviet state into a war machine. Part of the military-industrial complex had to be built in Siberia for security reasons. Stalin needed an enslaved workforce to implement this ambitious plan. He knew that the promise of turning the USSR into a great power would bring him the support of the Russian people in spite of all the hardships and repressions. The non-Russian peoples of the Soviet empire were less likely to support such a venture.

Moreover, among non-Russians, resistance to collectivization was especially strong. In the spring of 1930, uprisings against collectivization were numerous in Ukraine, the North Caucasus, the Cossack regions, and Azerbaijan. In Stalin's mind the national question was always inseparable from the peasant question. In 1925 he wrote: "The national question is essentially that of the peasantry" (Mace 79). Destroying the Ukrainian nation, which Stalin suspected would side with Poland in the event of a conflict between the USSR and its Western neighbours (Martin 327), became a priority. Stalin chose starvation deliberately as a means to attain this purpose. That Ukraine was specifically targeted is evident clearly in the different treatment that Transcaucasia (after the sacking of its old Bolsheviks) and Ukraine received. In a letter to Kaganovich on 17 August 1931, Stalin writes: "I understand now that Kartvelishvili [an old Georgian Bolshevik protected by Ordzhonikidze] and the secretariat of the Georgian Central Committee, by their mad policy of requisitioning grain, have caused famine in many parts of western Georgia. They do not understand that the methods of requisitions *necessary in the Ukrainian grain regions* [author's emphasis] are harmful in areas that are not producing grain and have no industrial proletariat.... We must accelerate the import of wheat, and immediately. Otherwise we will have riots, although the problem of grain supply is already solved here" (Khlevniuk et al. 51).

Hysteria about the so-called aggressive Polish designs against the USSR was used to justify the harsh treatment inflicted on Ukraine. A genocidal policy is always linked to a view of a world under siege: propaganda presents the eradication of the targeted group as a prophylactic measure. The blatant hypocrisy of Stalin's propaganda becomes clear when we take into account that a Soviet-Polish non-aggression pact was signed in July 1932. Moreover, the USSR was reinforcing its position on the international stage in other realms. In June 1932, Stalin learned from his spies that the Japanese had decided to avoid confrontation with the USSR. Additionally, Turkey—following destabilization in Transcaucasia caused by peasant uprisings—promised (in a secret protocol to the Soviet-Turkish treaty of 30 November 1931) to deport some of its most active political émigrés and to forbid anti-Soviet activity on Turkish territory (Balaev 236). Stalin's most draconian genocidal measures (i.e., the decision to confiscate seed grain) were introduced in Ukraine in December 1932. And in January 1933, starving peasants were ordered to stay in their villages and troops were deployed to prevent them from fleeing.

The Ukrainian elites were also targeted by Stalin. The joint plenum of the Central Committee and Central Executive Committee of the All-Union Communist Party (Bolsheviks), AUCP(B), held on 11 January 1933, launched a purge of the leadership of the Communist Party of Ukraine (CPU) and the end of the "Ukrainization" policy begun under Lenin. Stalin blamed the failure of the collective farms there on sabotage by "Petliurites," supporters of Ukrainian independence efforts in 1917–20 and then later in exile. Stalin depicted the exodus of hungry peasants as a Polish plot to discredit collectivization. After this Plenum the leadership of the CPU was replaced and six hundred political departments of Machine-Tractor Stations (MTS) were sent to Ukraine. "Dens of counter-revolutionaries" were unmasked in scientific and academic organizations.

As with the Jewish genocide organized by Himmler, the starvation of Ukraine was surrounded by the deepest secrecy. Vsevolod Balyts'kyi, chief of the state security service in Ukraine, writing to Genrikh Iagoda, chief of the All-Union OGPU, explained on 22 March 1933 that he requested his subordinates not to circulate written reports by the OGPU on the famine among Party secretaries. He asked to be informed personally by his subordinates through oral reports (Werth and Berelowitch 279–80).

The contemporary historiography of the Soviet Union has been shaped by a debate between the so-called "totalitarians" and the "revisionists." The totalitarian school, represented by such authors as Robert Conquest and Adam Ulam, emphasizes the role of ideology and terror in the Communist regime. It also stresses the role of Stalin as a decisive factor. The revisionists, which include Sheila Fitzpatrick and Jerry Hough, focus more on society and a "structuralist" approach. Documents made available after the collapse of the Soviet Union tend to vindicate the totalitarian interpretation. They prove that Stalin and the Soviet leadership were fully informed about the famine in Ukraine and that Stalin deliberately starved the Ukrainian population for ideological reasons: Peasants, especially Ukrainian ones, were too attached to private property and individual work, too contaminated by Western influence. Documents also show that local authorities repeatedly tried to mitigate the hard line imposed by Stalin, contrary to the theories of the revisionists who believed in "cumulative radicalization," that is, an amplifying role of the local bureaucracy, leading to total disaster. As a matter of fact, Stalin was constantly obliged to dispatch his closest associates to the provinces in order to impose his murderous policy on local Communists (as he would be forced to do later during the Great Purges).

All revolutionary regimes strive to implement irreversible measures. In Jacobin France, committing regicide, executing King Louis XVI, and later annexing Belgium, was perceived as crossing the Rubicon. Such acts isolated France from Europe, making total war inevitable and consolidated the revolutionary dictatorship. In the USSR the collectivization campaign and the ensuing Holodomor was such a Rubicon, with a similar goal of isolating the socialist fatherland by depopulating the borderlands. In Nazi Germany the "final solution" chained the German people to the sinking Hitler regime. Strikingly, the same expressions crop up in the justification of both the Nazi and Soviet crimes. According to the secretary of the Moscow Party organization, Karl Bauman, eradicating capitalism definitively in the countryside meant *"blow[ing] up the bridges so there is no way back* [author's emphasis]."[2] Goebbels, having been informed about the "Final Solution," writes in his *Journal* on 2 March 1943: "We have gone so far, especially in the Jewish question, that it is no longer possible to go back now. And it's better that way. *A movement and a people who have cut the bridges behind them fight more resolutely* [author's emphasis] than those who still have the possibility of going back" (Goebbels 78–79). On 14 November 1943 he noted, "[having] blown up the bridges ... We shall enter into history either as the greatest statesmen or the greatest criminals of all time."

I have tried to show in this paper how Stalin singlehandedly imposed his calamitous and criminal line on unenthusiastic followers and on resisting masses. We have seen that, as in Nazi Germany and later in Mao's China, radical nihilist policies were camouflaged by the stated ambition to build a great autarchic conquering empire. However, ultimately we still do not understand how a dictator can lead a whole people to self-destruction. The mystery remains.

Under the influence of social sciences, contemporary history tends to place emphasis on impersonal processes, on bureaucratic mechanisms, on mind-sets, on economic factors. This approach is likely a reflection of contemporary humanity, which feels overwhelmed by forces it does not control such as globalization, international finance, multinationals and the like. Reflection on totalitarian systems, paradoxically, should lead us to a more optimistic worldview: individual choices and individual actions count. Even more so, they are the main driving force. This means that moral categories, good and evil, are still relevant. Of course this can be shocking to our modern "non-judgmental" approach. The historian seeks to find the causes of human behaviour, to bestow intelligibility on the haphazard chaos of past events. In the chains of determinism that history brings to light, the student of past events always stumbles on a simple truth: ultimately man is

---

[2] See "Memorandum of 14 December 1929" (Danilov, vol. 2, 38).

free. The calamities of the twentieth century show that in our mass societies the will of an individual is more decisive than ever, especially when this individual is driven by evil coupled to a passion for absolute power. Economic factors, bureaucratic intricacies, inertia of traditions—these are of little weight when confronted with such a personality. Failure to understand these dynamics has left us blind to the dangers of modern despotic systems and explains our inability to address them in time.

WORKS CITED

Balaev, Aiyn. *Mamed Emin Rasulzade (1884-1955).* Moscow: Flinta, 2009. Print.

Charkviani, K. *Gantsdili da naazrevi.* Tbilisi: Merani, 2004. Print.

Conquest, Robert. *Sanglantes moissons: La collectivisation des terres en URSS.* Paris: Bouquin, 1995. Print.

Danilov, V. et al., eds. *Tragediia sovetskoi derevni. Kollektivizatsiia i raskulachivanie. Dokumenty i materialy v 5 tomakh, 1927-1939.* Moscow: Rosspen, 1999. Print.

Domenach, Jean-Luc. *Mao, sa cour et ses complots: derrière les Murs rouges*. Paris: Fayard, 2012. Print.

Furet, François, and Mona Ozouf. *Dictionnaire critique de la révolution française*: *Acteurs.* Paris: Flammarion, 1992. Print.

Getmanskii, A. E. "Politika Rossii v pol'skom voprose (60-e gody XIX veka)." *Voprosy istorii* 5 (2004): 24-45. Print.

Goebbels, Joseph, and Pierre Ayçoberry. *Journal, 1943-1945.* Paris: Tallandier, 2005. Print.

Ken, Oleg, and Aleksandr Rupasov. *Zapadnoe pogranichn'e: Politburo TsK VKP(b) i otnoshenia SSSR s zapadnymi sosednimi gosudarstvami, 1928-1934.* Moscow: Algoritm, 2014. Print.

Khaustov, V. N. et al., eds. *Lubianka: Stalin i NKVD-NKGD-GUKR "Smersh": 1939-mart 1946*: Moscow: Materik, 2006. Print.

Khlevniuk, O. V. et al., eds. *Stalin i Kaganovich: Perepiska 1931-1936 gg.* Moscow: Rosspen, 2001. Print.

Khlevniuk, O. V., Pierre Forgues, and Nicolas Werth. *Le cercle du Kremlin: Staline et le Bureau politique dans les années 30: Les jeux du pouvoir.* Paris: Éditions du Seuil, 1996. Print.

Kvashonkin, A. V. et al., eds. *Sovetskoe rukovodstvo. Perepiska 1928-1941.* Moscow: Rosspen, 1999. Print.

Mace, James E. "Soviet Man-Made Famine in Ukraine." *Century of Genocide.* Ed. S. Totten, W. Parsons, I. Charny. New York: Garland Publishing, 1995. 97-137. Print.

Martin, Terry. *The Affirmative Action Empire: Nations and Nationalism in the Soviet Union, 1923-1939.* Ithaca and London: Cornell UP, 2001. Print.

Sokolov, Boris. *Beria: Sud'ba vsesil'nogo narkoma.* Moscow: Veche, 2003. Print.

Souvarine, Boris. *Staline: Aperçu historique du bolchévisme.* Paris: Editions G. Lebovici, 1985. Print.

Stalin, Iosif. "Ob industrializatsii i khlebnoi probleme." *Polnoe sobranie sochinenii.* Vol. 11. n.d., n.p. *Iosif Vissarionovich Stalin. Sochineniia.* Web. 24 June 2014. <http://www.petrograd.biz/stalin/11-18.php>

Stalin, I. *Sochineniia.* Vol. 14. Moscow: Pisatel', 1997. Print.

Thom, F. *Beria, le Janus du Kremlin.* Paris: Cerf, 2013. Print.
Werth, Nicolas, and Alexis Berelowitch. *L'État soviétique contre les paysans. Rapports secrets de la police politique (Tcheka, GPR, NKVD), 1918-1939.* Paris: Tallandier, 2011. Print.

The Holodomor of 1932–33: How and Why?

Stanislav Kul'chyts'kyi
Ukrainian National Academy of Sciences (NANU), Institute of the History of Ukraine

Abstract: The study of the Ukrainian Holodomor is now sufficiently voluminous to establish the core concepts and events vital to its thorough scholarly understanding. This paper seeks to put forth one such possible outline. It briefly surveys the main sources upon which research on the topic relies and the major works pertinent to the development of scholarship on the Holodomor. This paper supports the position that the Holodomor was a genocide; it rebuts arguments against this position; and it examines the ways in which the Holodomor differs from the Holocaust, to which it is sometimes compared. By revealing the ideological and economic conditions of the Soviet Union under Joseph Stalin and the motivations of Stalin's leadership and his desire to eliminate the threat of Ukrainian nationalism to the Soviet state, this paper demonstrates how the Holodomor was made possible and why it took the course it did. The paper also examines how this deliberate famine was different from the All-Union famine that preceded it. Once the necessary components for understanding the Holodomor are determined, a coherent and truthful narrative about it can be established and the false narratives that deny the deliberate nature of the Famine can be revealed.

Keywords: Genocide, famine, Soviet Union, Joseph Stalin, Ukrainian nationalism

The number of works devoted to the Ukrainian Holodomor has surpassed twenty thousand titles. Over time, the topic has become overgrown with myths that impede our understanding of what really happened. Of course, the Holodomor is a complex topic, and it is practically impossible to describe within the scope of a single presentation how and why it occurred. However, it is possible and worthwhile to offer an outline so that specialists can either agree with the proposed theses or put forward substantiated objections.

STATEMENT OF THE PROBLEM

First and foremost, it is crucial to distinguish the All-Union famine of 1932–33 (which reached severe levels in the Ukrainian SSR during the first six months of 1932) from the Holodomor, when many Ukrainian villages were placed on "blacklists" as early as November 1932, and which saw a fifteen-fold increase in mortality in the republic from the previous year, claiming well over three million victims (Kul'chyts'kyi, *Chervonyi vyklyk* 517). The

All-Union famine was an undesired outcome for the Soviet Union, a crisis that had resulted from Stalin's socioeconomic policies. In contrast, the holodomors that took place in three Soviet commodity agriculture regions (the Ukrainian SSR, the North Caucasus krai [land or region], and the Lower Volga krai) were the consequence of large-scale Chekist actions aimed at the deliberate destruction of the peasants by starvation.[1]

The general public has come to view the Holocaust as a unique phenomenon and to employ a capital letter when using the term. This Jewish tragedy truly is unique because no state but the Third Reich devoted its resources to the targeted physical destruction of people solely because their ethnicity or religion differed from those of the majority.

The scale of the Ukrainian Holodomor is not commensurate with that of the Holocaust. Moreover, the ideology, circumstances, and motives behind murder carried out by the Stalinist state were different. All the same, it is possible to compare the Ukrainian Holodomor with the Holocaust in terms of killing on a mass scale, and there is value in examining the similarities between the two genocides without equating them.

Hitler's foundation was the National-Socialist ideology, and he proclaimed his intention to cleanse the "superior German race" of the "foreign Jewish substratum." Stalin's point of departure was a Communist ideology, based on the idea of class rather than nation. For Communist leaders, the superior class was the proletariat, that is, the working class, which was stripped of the means of production and thus completely dependent on the state.

In turning their intentions into reality, both Stalin and Hitler resorted to the physical destruction of people: Stalin was motivated by class considerations, while Hitler by the national. Class-based destruction led to the Holodomor; nation-based destruction led to the Holocaust. Since class cannot be squeezed into the framework of the nation (or the nation into the framework of class), the Holodomor as the consequence of the destruction of a class cannot be fit into the framework of the Holocaust, which was the consequence of the destruction of a nation.

These positions have an abstract and theoretical character, but it is impossible to proceed without them. The Ukrainian Holodomor must be analyzed simultaneously on two planes: how the Holodomor differed from the All-Union famine, which also affected Ukraine for a certain period of

---

[1] Ed. Note: The author has chosen to use the terms Cheka/Chekist throughout the essay in reference to the Soviet state security service of the day. We have chosen to leave it in this form.

time, and how the Ukrainian Holodomor differed from the holodomors that raged in those regions of the Soviet Union where the All-Union famine developed into a holodomor.

The use of the terms *holod* [famine] and *Holodomor* [murder by starvation] requires prior agreement about the fundamental difference between these terms. The concept *holod* is bound to an economic crisis that was for the Soviet government the undesirable result of a failure to replace commodity circulation by product exchange—in other words, the complete destruction of the free market. *Holodomor* refers to the punitive operation carried out by state security organs aimed at containing social disorder. The essence of this operation lay in the creation, in certain regions, of conditions that were incompatible with life, resulting in mass mortality from starvation, which was not only the predictable end of its punitive operation but desirable from the point of view of the government.

In continuing to distinguish the Holocaust and the Holodomor, I would like to pause and focus on the term that was introduced by Robert Conquest to characterize the famine of 1932–33 in the Soviet Union: terror-famine, that is, the killing of people by creating conditions incompatible with life.[2] Terror exists through the destruction of part of society in order to subordinate the entire society to the state, to compel it to do what the state wants, and also not do what the state does not desire. In other words, it is always a question of intimidating the majority by destroying a minority. Thus, one can say that terror was a method of state administration. Indeed, the proletarianization of society in the Soviet Union sparked furious resistance on the part of those population strata that owned private property. Famine and the holodomors in the USSR are connected to the collectivization of agriculture. Initially, the party of Lenin and Stalin destroyed the great landowners with the aid of the peasants, and, later, by means of collectivization, it set about destroying petty landowners, that is, the peasants.

Here I will embark on an analysis of the concrete historical subtext of the concepts of *holod* and *holodomor*. One is instantly struck by a fundamental difference between the Holodomor and the Holocaust. The Holocaust did not have the features of terror, that is, a brazen destruction of a part in order to attain the necessary behavior of the whole. In Nazi Germany the Jews were destroyed as an entire community. Researchers who, knowingly or unwittingly, deny the interpretation of the Ukrainian

---

[2] Ed. Note: This designation is used alternately with the phrase "terror by famine," which the author employs in the original Ukrainian text to this article.

Holodomor as terror by famine seek to study Soviet reality in the context of the utterly different realities of Nazi Germany.

The famine of 1932–33 was a taboo topic in the USSR until December 1987, but it was always studied in the Ukrainian diaspora. In the final years of the Soviet Union, Ukrainian, Russian, and Kazakh historians began to study this question intensively, but after 1991 it became unpopular in Russia and Kazakhstan. It is only thanks to the influence of rigorous study in Ukraine that Russian and Kazakh scholars are now resuming their research on this topic. Political circles in these states are placing substantial constraints on scholars, who are pressured to prove a) that regional famines were part of the All-Union famine, and nothing more; and b) that famine was not used by the state as a weapon, meaning that it was not an act of genocide.

However, the study of famine in 1932–33 in the USSR shows that the Soviet republics resisted, in varying degrees, the proletarianization of society ("the building of communism," in the parlance of this period). Furthermore, this resistance represented varying degrees of danger for the state, which was implementing the proletarianization. For that reason, terror-famine was not applied everywhere. Soviet Ukraine was always at the mercy of many forms of terror. It was precisely in Ukraine that the most horrific form of terror—terror by famine—was applied. However, this does not mean that this brand of terror did not exist in other regions of the USSR.

In Ukraine, terror by famine was the result of the confluence of certain circumstances of place and time. However, this does not mean that the concept of the genocide of the Ukrainian people, i.e., the Holodomor, must be extended to encompass the entire period of Soviet rule or the period of Stalinist dictatorship.

Is it useful to examine the Kremlin's actions that caused the Ukrainian Holodomor in the context of the UN Convention on the Prevention and Punishment of Genocide, adopted on 9 December 1948. To date such attempts have failed to convince many. Communist transformations required the destruction, at times even physical, of population strata that were tied to private ownership. When it was claimed that the victims of the genocide were exclusively Ukrainians as a national group, citing the groups enumerated in the UN Convention (racial, ethnic, national, and religious), protests came forth from Russian researchers. It is no accident that social groups were deleted from the original text of the Convention as a result of efforts by Stalin's diplomats. Even Russians in the USSR were viewed as a social group. Further to this, researchers from the Russian Federation who know that Russians were also victims of genocide are not willing to risk a conflict with the post-Soviet government, which has not shifted far enough ideologically and mentally from the Soviet government to recognize the genocide that was committed against its very own people.

Famine in 1932–33 in the USSR has become a subject of study throughout the world. Sooner or later, thanks to the force of irrefutable facts, the international community will issue a legal assessment of the Stalinist terror-famine, which by its very nature was genocidal. Perhaps the UN Convention on Genocide will be amended. In the meantime, however, it is essential to unite around Robert Conquest's conclusion that ends the chapter "A Land Laid Waste" of his 1986 book *The Harvest of Sorrow*:

> But whether these events are to be formally defined as genocide is scarcely the point. It would hardly be denied that a crime has been committed against the Ukrainian nation; and, whether in the execution cellars, the forced labour camps, or the starving villages, crime after crime against the millions of individuals forming that nation. (Conquest 272–73)

In 1989 the British historian Alec Nove noted that in his polemics with Conquest he posited that Stalin's blow was aimed against the peasantry, which included many Ukrainians, rather than against Ukrainians per se, many of whom were peasants (Nove 170). Since then, historians have sought to determine whom Stalin was really liquidating, Ukrainians or peasants. This polemic has been somewhat shaped by scholars who define the Holodomor via the Holocaust. For example, the Ukrainian-language version of Vasyl' Hryshko's book *The Ukrainian Holocaust of 1933* first appeared in New York in 1978. In Kyiv this was the title given to the immense nine-volume collection of famine survivor testimonies, which Iurii Mytsyk began publishing in 2003. It was thought that this evocative title might spur recognition for the Holodomor as an act of genocide. But Ukrainians do not have the moral right to use the concept of the Holocaust in the figurative sense. The Ukrainian Holocaust is the destruction of 1.6 million Jews in Ukraine during the Second World War. Furthermore, equating the Holodomor with the Holocaust is the equivalent of claiming that Ukrainians were persecuted in the same way as Jews were on Nazi-occupied territories, wherever and whenever they were found. The absurdity of such a claim is obvious, as is the claim that the Stalinist regime imprisoned or destroyed peasants whenever and wherever it found them. If the Holodomor in Ukraine was the result of coinciding, concrete circumstances, they must be studied.

According to conventional wisdom, famine in the early 1930s was caused by grain requisitioning. And these requisitions were the cause of the All-Union famine. The holodomors were a result of a Chekist operation that consisted of two chronologically distinct sets of actions: initially, the confiscation of remaining grain, and in general the confiscation of all existing foodstuffs during searches of farmyards; and, later, after a break intended to last a few weeks, the provisioning of grain from state reserves to collective farms and state farms in the starving regions in the form of an apparent loan for the purpose of organizing the spring sowing. The government's actions were not aimed at the destruction by starvation of the entire rural population in the regions that had been utterly stripped of food. Those who were dying were meant to convince the living that it was crucial to work conscientiously on collective farms. This terror-famine did not differ from other types of terror, in which the imprisonment or destruction of a certain number of citizens was used in order to obtain obedience from the rest of the population.

The confiscations by the Chekists were masked by state grain deliveries, whose relief for the starving regions was broadly publicized. Has the confiscation aspect been duly reflected in the historical literature? Let us take, for example, Davies' and Wheatcroft's 2004 monograph on the history of famine in 1931–33 (reissued in Russian in 2011; see Davies and Wheatcroft). The authors list and annotate 56 Party and government resolutions concerning grain relief to the starving regions, which were issued during the first half of 1933. Ukraine received 176,200 tons, the North Caucasus—88,500, and the Lower Volga region—15,500; all other regions received a total of 39,800 tons. The actions of the Central Committee of the All-Union Communist Party of Bolsheviks [AUCP(B)], caught "in a desperate situation," are described in detail, but those who created that situation remain nameless.[3]

The relief provided to the starving is regarded as a convincing argument pointing to the government's lack of intent to use famine for the purpose of destroying the population. Several years ago the Archival Agency of the Russian Federation published a collection of colour photocopies of Kremlin documents on famine-related questions. Readers of this large-format book can not only familiarize themselves with the contents of declassified documents but also see what they look like. Among the documents—complete with the red seal of the AUCP(B) Central Committee and the scrawling signature of the General Secretary in black ink—are resolutions adopted by the Politburo of the Central Committee of the AUCP(B) on 8 February 1933, concerning the provision of 700,000 poods of rye "for the food needs of workers of state farms, MTSs, and MTMs,[4] as well as leading (Party and non-Party) activists on collective

---

[3] Davies and Wheatcroft 214–24 (texts), 479–85 (tables).
[4] MTS=Machine-Tractor Station; MTM=Machine-Tractor Shop.

farms" in North Caucasus krai and Dnipropetrovsk and Odesa oblasts (Antipova and Pigarev 244). If you divide the food relief issued to Ukraine (1,762,000 tons) by the total number of rural inhabitants, each person would have received an average of no more than half a pood of grain for a six-month period; meanwhile, relief was provided mainly to "leading Party and non-Party activists."

THE DOCTRINAL ROOTS OF THE ALL-UNION FAMINE

The regional holodomors emerged against the background of the All-Union famine. It must be ascertained why people began dying of starvation during the years when the colossal structures of heavy industry were being constructed. In the introduction to the Russian edition of his book on the famine, Stephen Wheatcroft commented: "R. Davies and I did not find any evidence that the Soviet government was carrying out a program of genocide against Ukraine" (Davies and Wheatcroft 12). Indeed, there never was any such program, nor was there any program for organizing an All-Union famine. But the Bolshevik leaders were pursuing a definite program as they undertook the creation of a socioeconomic order that was unprecedented in history.

Arguably, the most fundamental work on this topic is the twenty-volume set of monographs on the formation of the Soviet system in 1917–1937, the work of the Birmingham-based school of historical economics, which included Edward Carr, his pupil Robert Davies, and Davies' pupil Stephen Wheatcroft. Carr suspended his work on the fourteenth volume because the period after 1928 could not be researched without archival sources to which he had no access. Other members of the school completed six volumes based on archival materials.

However, the Birmingham school, as well as other historians, studied only what had happened, while the creation of the Soviet system lay outside natural historical processes. A system was created in the Soviet Union that was the product of subjective notions. Therefore, it is also crucial to study that which did not happen in this state—that which did not happen because it turned out to be unrealizable. The above-mentioned book about the famine by Davies and Wheatcroft contains an immense quantity of facts, but it ignores the Bolshevik Party program that turned upside down the ideas of two young men who, in the stormy atmosphere of 1847, were inspired to formulate the fiery sentences of the "Manifesto of the Communist Party."

Vladimir Lenin returned to Russia from emigration in April 1917 with the intention of transforming a people's revolution into a communist one. The theses of the Bolshevik leader, published in *Pravda*, outlined not only a plan to seize power but also a course of further action, such as changing the name of the party (from social-democratic to communist), adopting a Communist Party program, creating a commune state, and founding an international organization of communist parties, the Comintern. The Bolsheviks' communist doctrine was based on revolutionary Marxism of the mid-nineteenth century. In their "Manifesto of the Communist Party," Karl Marx and Friedrich Engels summarized their views in one short sentence: "Communists can express their theory with one principle: the elimination of private property" (Marks [Marx] and Enhel's [Engels] 4: 422). The manifesto emphasized that the revolutionary proletariat had to expropriate the bourgeoisie and centralize all means of production in the hands of "the state, that is, the proletariat, organized as the ruling class" (Marks and Enhel's 4: 429).

The Leninist party program partially coincided with the demands put forward by the soviets of workers' and soldiers' deputies, the most influential force during the Russian Revolution. From his first day back in Russia, Lenin issued the slogan "All power to the Soviets!" With the aid of terror and propaganda, the Bolsheviks eliminated competing parties from the soviets, transformed these councils into clones of their own party, and turned them into organs of authority. That is how Soviet power emerged; a symbiosis between the Bolshevik-led political dictatorship and the administrative power of the organs of the soviets. As a result of the Party's reconstruction on the principles of "democratic centralism," that is, the blind subordination of lower links to the higher, all power was concentrated in the hands of the leaders. Horizontal-type organizations that existed in society, on the basis of which a civil society had been formed, were either destroyed or vertically integrated, that is, converted to the principle of "democratic centralism."

The vertical structure of the Party and the soviets rooted itself in society with the help of "transmission belts," a ramified system of soviets, Komsomol branches, trade unions, and various types of civic organizations. The Bolsheviks' party was also transformed into a "transmission belt," once an internal party of leaders (the *nomenklatura*) was formed within it. Over time, the vertical of state security was removed from the supervision of local Party committees and placed under the direct control of the General Secretary of the CC (Central Committee) of AUCP(B). Just like the Party and Soviet verticals, it penetrated society in the form of hundreds of thousands of its "secret collaborators" in Ukraine, numbering in the millions throughout the USSR as a whole. In contrast to all preceding social orders, Soviet society was a skeleton consisting of a system of state organs. As a result, it behaved like a hierarchized, Party- or army-type structure. From April 1917 onwards this skeleton acquired a name: the commune state. True, in everyday life the communist state was called the worker-peasant or

Soviet state. Unlike traditional democratic or totalitarian states that were disconnected from their societies, the communist-type state burrowed itself into its society through every institution, which imbued it with colossal power. Only this type of state was capable of realizing all that required realization in a communist utopia, specifically: expropriation of society and supplementation of political dictatorship with economic dictatorship.

Marx, who devoted his life to studying the societies in which he lived, never rejected the ideas enshrined in the "Manifesto of the Communist Party." His proposal to divide communism into two phases, according to the distribution of material benefits, became known after his death as socialism, in which distribution takes places according to labor; and full communism, in which the worker receives benefits according to his needs. As Marx emphasized, under the category of the production of benefits, communist-socialism (there were other, non-Marxist, notions of the socialist order) did not differ from full communism. The maturing of socialism (according to Marx) or its construction (according to Lenin) was linked to the destruction of private property and the conversion of the ownership of the means of production as well the replacement of the circulation of currency by the direct distribution of products, depending on the contribution of one's labour.

Every Bolshevik leader until the time of Nikita Khrushchev assured his generation of citizens that communism, with its distribution according to need, was no longer a distant dream. In order to hasten the "bright future," it was useful to reconcile oneself to the temporary difficulties encountered in the process of building socialism. But in Lenin's and Stalin's time (until 1933), the commune state sought to create a society that had rid itself of private property, a free market, and commodity-monetary relations.

The logic behind the communist transformations required the simultaneous elimination of private property owned by large and petty landowners. It turned out to be a comparatively simple matter to remove the bourgeoisie from production, although the Bolsheviks had to endure a civil war. They had the support of the working class, which had gained fundamental rights in the management of nationalized property. The transformations in the countryside were connected with the organization of Soviet enterprises (state farms) on the basis of landowners' estates, as well as communes, through the unification of peasant farmsteads. Having at its disposal factories, state farms, and communes, the commune state was given an opportunity, so the Bolshevik leaders thought, to liquidate the market and introduce direct exchange of products in place of commodity circulation. It was precisely these transformations that were demanded by the program adopted by the Russian Communist Party (Bolshevik) in March 1919.

However, the peasants and soldiers mobilized from rural areas did not wish to listen to any talk of state farms and communes, and they demanded an equal distribution of land. The Council of People's Commissars (*Sovnarkom*, or SNK), headed by Lenin, was thus forced to accede to these demands, and he was then faced with the critical need to seek, in place of the product exchange between the city and the countryside, other ways of transforming the earning wages of workers in nationalized sectors into material means of subsistence. Under the existing conditions, the government banned free trade and introduced among peasants obligatory tasks in order to meet state production needs.

Taken aback by the introduction of the surplus appropriation system (*prodrazverstka*) in 1919, the peasants began to limit their sowing plots to their own needs, as they were loath to work for the state without material compensation. Then, in December 1920, Lenin supplemented the food appropriation system with a sowing one. State organs emerged in the Soviet republics with the purpose of informing every farmstead about the sowing plan and monitoring how scrupulously the peasants carried out the sowing in order to obtain a harvest that would be handed over to the state. What emerged was something akin to the "lessons" that had been learned by the serf-owning landowners, which raised the threat of a civil war involving the entire peasantry. Lenin came to his senses and introduced the New Economic Policy (NEP), and a few months before his death he began calling upon the Party to repudiate its obsolete views of socialism.

After Stalin's successful five-year struggle for power over the Party's ruling elite, he formulated two theses that were enshrined in resolutions adopted at the Fifteenth Congress of the AUCP(B) held in December 1927: the necessity of collectivizing agriculture and of transforming commodity circulation between the city and the countryside into an exchange of products. In organizing the switch to all-out collectivization, on 26 August 1929, the Central Committee of the AUCP(B) issued a resolution entitled "About the Main Conclusions and Immediate Tasks in the Branch of the Contractual System of Grain Sowing," which approved the new principles of economic relations with the peasantry. The contractual agreement between the state and the peasantry began to be viewed as a "method of organizing systematic product exchange between the city and the countryside" (Kuz'mina and Sharova 196–97).

The Bolshevik leaders realized the danger of the surplus appropriation system: the peasants were sowing less and less, while the state was requisitioning an increasingly larger proportion of the harvest, the absolute dimensions of which were shrinking with every passing year. The threat of famine loomed over both the countryside that was being looted and over the cities, which relied on grain supplies issued through the ration card system. However, Stalin anticipated that the peasants, who had been driven into collective farms, would no longer be allowed to decide how much they should sow. At the Sixteenth Congress of the Communist Party in June 1930, he declared optimistically that thanks to the collective farm order that had been established in the country, the grain problem was being resolved successfully (Stalin 12: 285–86).

But the General Secretary miscalculated. The peasants' disinterest in farming was leading to immense grain losses during the sowing, harvesting, and transporting periods. The CP(B)U (Communist Party (Bolsheviks) of Ukraine) leaders estimated the losses of the 1931 harvest at between 120 and 200 million poods, that is, up to one half of the annual food stock of the republic's rural population (Kul'chyts'kyi, "Sozdanie" 643). In order to wrest the increasingly diminishing production from collective farms, the state was forced to decrease the export of grain, the proceeds of which were to pay for the equipment needed to construct new industrial installations. Famine also emerged in cities because the state was decreasing grain supply quotas or removing certain population categories from supply lists.

Correcting Notions of Communist-Socialism

The famine that took place in the early 1920s was the result of a breakdown of the economy, a catastrophic drought, and two years of increased appropriations. A drought exacerbated the shrinking sowing acreage, and this shrinkage was the peasants' reaction to the confiscation of agricultural produce that had taken place during the surplus appropriations of 1919–20. The excessive appropriations of 1929–32 led to similar consequences, but they appeared at a slower pace because the sowing acreage on collective farms was not shrinking but increasing.

It seemed as though by creating collective farms the commune state was securing the possibility of distributing output without market participation, as per the demands of the theory pursued by the leaders of the AUCP(B). In the 1918 "Program of the Communists (Bolsheviks)," Nikolai Bukharin painted the following picture:

> The task does not consist of every peasant pottering about a small work plot, like the manure beetle on his mound, but of poor peasants switching to community labor in as large numbers as possible. How to do this? This can and must be done by two routes: first of all, by the comradely farming of former large landowners' estates; second, by the organization of laboring agricultural communes. (Bukharin 59)

However, in the standoff between the state and the peasantry, Stalin was forced to organize collective farms in the form of cooperative associations (*arteli*), not communes. Once the members of collective farms became convinced that the state was distributing the output of these cooperative associations in such a way that it was slipping out of their hands, they concentrated their efforts on tending to their own private plots. In the fields that belonged to collective farms, grain losses went above critical levels. Despite efforts of American sovietologist Mark Tauger, who has devoted much of his career to determining the scale of the 1932 harvest, we do not know the extent of the losses. The terrible specter of famine appeared as early as 1931, initially in Kazakhstan, where collectivization took the barbaric form of sedentarization, that is, the forcible settling of a nomadic people.

As noted earlier, Lenin had planned to supplement the food appropriation system with a sowing system and to liquidate the circulation of currency. However, after several weeks of reflection, he introduced a food tax instead of appropriations, thus recognizing the right of peasants to their own output, and shortly afterwards he renounced all attempts to introduce communist-socialism in its complete form. Stalin, however, refused for an entire year to heed the advice of the other Party leaders to follow Lenin's example.

It is worth looking at the advice that was dispensed under pressure from the growing economic crisis. In their speeches at the Seventeenth Party Conference (January–February 1932), Aleksei Stetskii, head of the Department for Agitation and Propaganda (Agitprop) at the CC AUCP(B), and Boris Sheboldaev, the North Caucasus Party secretary, called money and trade "holdovers from the old society." However, a speech delivered by Valerian Kuibyshev, head of Gosplan USSR and deputy head of the Sovnarkom, and a corresponding conference resolution expressed the conviction that at the current stage it was impossible to replace trade by direct product exchange (XVII konferentsiia VKP[b] 180, 193, 211). In a note prepared for the Central Committee in January 1932, Jan Rudzutak, head of the Central Control Commission of the AUCP(B) and People's Commissar of the Workers' and Peasants' Inspection of the USSR, insisted on the need to inform collective farms about the state grain delivery plan already at the beginning of the year. The peasants would have every reason to bring in a good harvest, Rudzutak convinced Stalin, if they were certain that they would be able to keep their surplus production for themselves. In a note to Stalin dated 15 March 1932, Stanislav Kosior proposed a different form of surplus appropriation:

> To announce in the name of Union organizations the order of grain deliveries from the future harvest based on the fact that the larger the harvest achieved by the collective farm and the collective farm member, the

larger the reserves it will be able to issue and distribute for personal consumption. (Ivnitskii 336)

On 20 May 1932, the Central Executive Committee (TsVK) and the Sovnarkom of the USSR issued a resolution on collective farm trade, which promised to allow the peasants to sell grain freely after they had met their grain quotas. This promise was made in order to create favorable conditions for state grain deliveries. Oleg Khlevniuk, the brilliant scholar of Stalinist documents, has noted that the General Secretary mentioned market trade only in the context of the struggle against "speculators and resellers," but he was attracted to the idea of supplying the countryside with consumer goods by means of the contract system (Khlevniuk 131). Khlevniuk does not explain the reason for this, but it is easily understood in the light of Bolshevik notions of building relations between the city and the countryside on the principles of product exchange.

On 19 June 1932, Vlas Chubar, the head of the Soviet Ukrainian government, wrote a letter to Viacheslav Molotov and Joseph Stalin, expressing his apprehensions concerning the new harvest. He warned: "In order [for the peasants] to better secure themselves for the winter compared to last year, they'll begin the mass theft of grain." Chubar's use of the word "theft" was not accidental: the Party leaders regarded the output of collective farms as the property of the state, not of collective farm members. That same day Hryhorii Petrovs'kyi, the head of the All-Ukrainian Central Executive Committee (VUTsVK), warned Molotov and Stalin: "Because of starvation the peasants will be gathering unripened grain, and much of it may perish in vain" (Khlevniuk 188). The Soviet security organs, monitoring the situation in the Ukrainian countryside, also reported to Stalin that the peasants were complaining that they had handed over the 1931 harvest to the state and were now prepared to fight for the grain, which they considered their own property, not that of the state (Danilov, Manning and Viola 3: 403-4).

Reacting to these reports on 20 July, Stalin, who was vacationing at a health resort, wrote to Lazar Kaganovich and Viacheslav Molotov in the Kremlin about the need to adopt a two-pronged law, commonly referred to as the "five ears of grain law," that would a) make collective farm and cooperative property equivalent to state property; and b) punish theft of property by handing down sentences of at least ten years (even though formally the law called for a death penalty). Without such measures, which the General Secretary himself called "draconian," it would be impossible, in his view, to strengthen the collective farm system. Beginning in 1930, various government departments set about devising measures aimed at the organizational and economic strengthening of collective farms that were being built by exploiting the material interests of rural workers. However, in his letters to the Kremlin written in July, Stalin demanded only one thing: "Finish off and bury... individualistic and loudmouth habits, practices, and traditions" (Khlevniuk 235, 240-41). On 7 August 1932, the TsVK and SNK USSR adopted the resolution "On Safekeeping Property of State Enterprises, Collective Farms and Cooperatives and Strengthening Public (Socialist) Property," the points of which were an exact reiteration of the punitive measures formulated by Stalin (Rudych and Pyrih 308).[5]

The state grain deliveries of the 1932 harvest were fraught with difficulties. In October Stalin created extraordinary grain procurement commissions: Molotov, the head of the Soviet government, was dispatched to Ukraine armed with dictatorial powers; Kaganovich, the secretary of the CC AUCP(B), was sent to the North Caucasus; and Pavel Postyshev, the secretary of the CC AUCP(B), was dispatched to the Lower Volga krai. Party and Soviet resolutions bearing the identical title "Concerning Measures for Accelerating the State Grain Deliveries," were authored by Molotov, agreed to by Stalin, and signed by Kosior and Chubar. They put forward the demand "to organize the confiscation of grain pilfered during harvesting, threshing, and transporting" (Mykhailychenko, Shatalina, and Kul'chyts'kyi 548). Collective farms and members of the farms who failed to complete the assigned tasks were to be issued fines in kind (meat and potatoes).

In November Vsevolod Balyts'kyi, deputy head of the OGPU and special OGPU plenipotentiary for the Ukrainian SSR, was dispatched to Ukraine. On the heels of Stalin's latest instructions, Balyts'kyi issued his first instructions to the GPU of the Ukrainian SSR, confirming the existence in Ukraine of the "organized sabotage of state grain deliveries and the fall sowing, organized mass thefts on collective farms and state·farms, terror [directed] at the most steadfast and staunch Communists and activists in the countryside, the influx of dozens of Petliurite emissaries, and the distribution of Petliurite leaflets." On the basis of this political diagnosis, a conclusion was reached about the "unambiguous existence in Ukraine of an organized, counter-revolutionary, insurgent underground that is connected with foreign countries and foreign intelligence services, primarily the Polish general staff." Finally, the following task was assigned:

> The exposure and smashing of the counter-revolutionary, insurgent underground and the infliction of a decisive blow at all counter-revolutionary, kulak-Petliurite elements that are actively counteracting and

---

[5] An excerpt of the text, in English translation, can be found in Klid and Motyl 239.

disrupting the chief measures of Soviet power and the party of peasants in the countryside (Shapoval and Zolotar'ov 189).

The specter of famine loomed over the peasants, who were being stripped of the last remnants of the harvest, and over the residents of cities, whom the state was unable to feed. Even those strata of the population that the Chekists called "socially close" were beginning to constitute a threat to Stalin and his associates. Some second-echelon leaders began to regard Stalin's implementation of the CC AUCP(B)'s general line as a threat to the Party and the state. But the General Secretary did not stray from the chosen course, regarding the peasants' natural disinclination to work without material compensation as *sabotage*. Their desire to retain a portion of the harvest (even that which was grown by independent farmers on their plots of land) was regarded as *theft*. The intent of local government and collective farm leaders to conceal grain from state grain delivery officials in order to avert famine was characterized as *counter-revolution*.

On 27 November 1932, Stalin convened a joint meeting of the Politburo of the CC and the Presidium of the Central Control Commission of the AUCP(B) in order to censure a number of Russian government leaders who held the General Secretary personally responsible for the failure of the state grain deliveries. He explained that the failure was a result of the "penetration of collective farms and state farms by anti-Soviet elements for the purpose of organizing wrecking and sabotage." Stalin emphasized: "It would be unwise if the Communists, seeing as collective farms are a socialist form of the economy, did not respond to the blow of these individual members of collective farms and collective farms with a shattering blow" (Danilov, Manning and Viola 3: 559). The Russian phrase *sokrushitel'nyi udar* was not transcribed. The phrase "individual members of collective farms and collective farms" figured in a stenographic report circulated to low-ranking Party committees. Stalin spoke more frankly at a meeting of higher Party leaders, naming regions where the extraordinary grain delivery commissions were operating and called concrete enemies White Guardists and Petliurites (Anderson, 3: 589, 657–58).

Seven weeks after promising "to respond with a shattering blow" against "saboteurs," "thieves," and "counter-revolutionaries," Stalin realized that this was not possible without economic methods of overcoming the economic catastrophe. On 19 January 1933, the SNK USSR and the CC AUCP(B) adopted the resolution "Concerning the Obligatory Delivery of Grain to the State by Collective Farms and Independent Farms." The switch from the contractual system, with its extensible state grain deliveries, to a tax in kind allowed the peasants to determine even before the beginning of the sowing campaign the quantity of grain they were obliged to hand over to the state in the fall. Now they had to be concerned with preventing losses that affected the decrease only of their portion of the harvest.

This is what lay on the surface of the relationship between the peasantry and the state. But the essence of this reform went much deeper. Unlike in other spheres of the economy, the commune state did not absorb agriculture but recognized its autonomy. In using the surplus appropriation system as a method of conducting economic relations with the countryside, it managed the distribution of production like a private owner. Meanwhile, the tax on foodstuffs signaled the state's recognition of the producer's private ownership of output and the state's agreement to lay claim only to a fixed proportion of this output in the form of a tax.

The possibility of using their output at their own discretion after settling accounts with the state meant that the peasants not only could consume it but also exchange it for goods through purchasing and selling. Nearly all essential goods were manufactured in the state sector of the economy. Therefore, the state's economic dealings with collective farms, collective farm members, and independent farmers (above all, by state sector employees who received wages and wanted to convert them to agricultural goods) took place on the basis of commodity circulation, not product exchange, that is, through a free market with prices that were formed on the basis of the law of supply and demand. Naturally, this market had to have a respectable name: the collective farm. As of 1933 collective farms acquired a form that was forever remembered by the citizens of the former Soviet Union.

It appeared that Stalin had changed the notion of communo-socialism that he was building. Like Lenin in his time, Stalin stopped at the border separating the utopia that had been achieved with the aid of terror and propaganda from the utopia that could not be created at any cost. Goods and monetary relations, as well as a market, were to remain in the USSR. The General Secretary imperceptibly linked the need to establish product exchange instead of commodity circulation with the second phase of communism. This allowed him to proclaim the victory of socialism as early as the mid-1930s, and during the preparation of his *Works* in the postwar period, Stalin introduced crucial corrections into the texts of articles that had been published in 1929–32.[6]

---

[6] See, for example, my book *Holodomor* 212–13.

THE TECHNOLOGY OF THE "SHATTERING BLOW"

The essence of the Chekist operation lay in the confiscation of foodstuffs in the starving countryside, an operation that took the form of searches of peasant farmsteads. Stalin saw to this in a telegram sent on 1 January 1933 to the leaders of the Ukrainian SSR in Kharkiv. The first point of the message requested village councils to order all members of collective farms and independent farmers to hand over voluntarily to the state "grain pilfered earlier and concealed." The second point of the telegram concerned those who ignored this demand: "With regard to collective farm members, collective farms, and independent farmers who are stubbornly continuing to conceal pilfered grain that is being hidden from stock-taking, the most severe punishment measures will be applied, as foreseen by the resolution of the TsVK and SNK USSR dated 7 August 1932 ("On Safekeeping Property of State Enterprises, Collective Farms and Cooperatives and Strengthening Public [Socialist] Property") (Rudych and Pyrih 308, Klid and Motyl 239). The connection between the first and second point prompted the government to organize a search of every peasant farmstead. The threat of applying the "five ears of grain" law (mentioned above) to any peasant who refused to give the state "pilfered and concealed grain" could be carried out only when it was determined that he was indeed refusing.

The confiscation of all foodstuffs during the course of these searches demolishes the arguments of those who oppose calling the Holodomor genocide. That is why they always demand documents as proof. But these terrible intentions could not be recorded in writing. This was a conviction of Soviet leaders, and their point of view is corroborated by various documents. In November 1932, the Starominsk raion committee of the AUCP(B) in the North Caucasus krai adopted the following resolution concerning the inhabitants of a nearby village: "Apply the severest means of influence and coercion in carrying out the confiscation of all food products." The resolution drew the attention of Molotov, who in a letter to Mendel Khataevich, secretary of the CC CP(B)U, hypocritically called it "un-Bolshevik" and stemming from "despair, for which we have no grounds." Molotov emphasized that the resolution cast a shadow on the policies of the Party, which was opposed to the local government practice of "taking any kind of grain and wherever it wants, without accounting for it, et cetera" (Kondrashin 216). It must be noted here that Molotov was talking only about grain. This product was of strategic importance because the state was obliged to feed the urban population. But in the given instance, the issue was not about grain—because, after all, the residents of that village no longer had any—nor even about meat and potatoes (which were listed in the legislation about fines in kind drafted by Molotov himself), but about all foodstuffs without exception. A famine caused by grain appropriations could have been rationalized by any number of excuses, for example, by the crucial need to create a defense infrastructure in anticipation of the events that would occur in 1941. In fact, such rationales are often invoked when the Ukrainian genocide is denied. But when a state confiscates not just grain but every kind of food, its intentions should be characterized as murderous; there simply cannot be any other explanation. The issue here is a preplanned mass murder that was carried out professionally, and not just of people whom the Kremlin deemed as saboteurs, but women, children, and the elderly. On a signal from Stalin, local activists and local members of Committees of Poor Peasants carried out searches and confiscations of all foodstuffs under the supervision of Chekists. The underprivileged were starving and did not have to be persuaded to engage in these activities.

Holodomor survivors have described these confiscations. Hundreds of statements have been recorded and published in which eyewitnesses describe how the search brigades took not just meat and potatoes but every scrap of food. The "Mapa: Digital Atlas of Ukraine" project (http://gis.huri.harvard.edu/) currently being undertaken by the Harvard Ukrainian Research Institute focuses first on the Holodomor and will feature a map of the location of eyewitnesses who corroborated the confiscation of all foodstuffs on the territory of the Ukrainian SSR and the North Caucasus krai. This map will become a full-fledged document, not someone's subjective view.

The "shattering blow" was a secret operation, even though it affected a huge swathe of territory. The secrecy was specific: the death-dealing famine could be mentioned only in the top-secret documents of Party and state organs, called "special files." No officials of any rank were permitted to utter aloud the word "famine," which precluded the possibility of any discussion on this topic, but with the aid of these "special files" and with their exceptional status governing use and storage, they could implement measures that the general famine demanded of them.

Famine could not have been a secret to the millions of peasants who were starving. How did officials talk to them at the height of the Holodomor? During the First All-Union Congress of Collective-Farm Shock Workers, held in February 1933, the People's Commissar of Agriculture of the USSR Iakov Iakovlev accused Ukrainian collective farm members of having failed to gather the 1932 harvest properly, as a result of which "they inflicted damage on the government and on themselves." He did not explain this "damage to themselves" but summarized the issue thus: "And from this, comrades-Ukrainian collective farm members, we will draw the conclusion: The time has come to pay for the bad work in the past" (*Pravda*, 19 February 1933). The regional congresses of collective-farm shock workers, held by the CC AUCP(B), concluded with an All-Union Congress, which was attended by Stalin. His speech was utterly cynical: "Lenin, our great teacher, said: 'He who does not work shall not eat.' What does this mean? Against whom were Lenin's words directed? Against exploiters, against those who do not work themselves but compel others to work, and they enrich themselves at other people's expense. And against whom else? Against those who idle and want to live at others' expense" (Stalin 13: 248).

In addition to an information blackout, a physical blockade of repressed regions was organized. On 22 January 1932, Stalin wrote a letter in his own hand to the CC AUCP(B) and SNK USSR (the original is extant) about putting a stop to the mass exodus of peasants from Ukraine and the Kuban to other regions. On 16 February this directive was circulated throughout the Lower Volga krai (Danilov, Manning, and Viola 3: 32, 635, 644).

There is a definite consistency to the actions that transformed the All-Union famine into regional holodomors:

- The creation by Stalin of extraordinary state grain delivery commissions in the three regions of highly marketable agriculture;
- The introduction, on Stalin's initiative, of legislation concerning fines in kind in the event of the failure of peasants to return "pilfered and concealed grain";
- The organizing, in accordance with Stalin's New Year's telegram, of universal searches of nonexistent reserves of "pilfered and concealed grain";
- The confiscation during searches of all storable foodstuffs;
- The physical blockading of regions that were utterly stripped of food;
- The ban (enforced until December 1987) on using the word "famine" in the USSR in connection with famine in 1932–33.

We also have the result of this consistency of action: an excess mortality of the population. According to the latest estimates compiled by a team of specialists at the Institute of Demography and Social Studies of the National Academy of Sciences of Ukraine (headed by Oleh Wolowyna, a professor at the University of North Carolina at Chapel Hill), the excess mortality rate in the rural regions of the Ukrainian SSR in 1932 was 207,000; 3,335,000 in 1933; and in the cities—43,000 and 194,000, respectively (Kul'chyts'kyi, *Chervonyi vyklyk* 517).

According to the Russian scholar Viktor Kondrashin, the scale of the Ukrainian famine was comparable to the scope of famine in Russia's grain-producing regions. He concurs with Stephen Wheatcroft, who estimates the number of famine victims in Ukraine in the range of 3.5 to 4 million, and in the USSR as a whole—between 6 and 7 million (Kondrashin 245). However,

Kondrashin cites these figures, which indeed reflect the real number of victims, in order to substantiate the following viewpoint: "Stalin did not have the idea of destroying the Ukrainian people and Ukraine with the aid of 'terror' and 'genocide' by famine" (Kodrashin 242). This is true; there was no such "idea"; in this the Ukrainian Holodomor differs fundamentally from the Holocaust. However, the purposeful and cold-blooded destruction of millions of peasants, which warrants the legal description of genocide, took place both in Ukraine and in Russia. In Kondrashin's fact-filled monograph we find various data not connected by a single topic on the confiscation of all foodstuffs; on the information blackout; and on the physical blockade of the Lower Volga region, as well as on the end result of this Chekist operation: the stark decline in the rural population as evidenced by the 1937 census in comparison with the 1926 census. After this holodomor the Lower Volga krai was divided into three parts: Saratov oblast (where the rural population had shrunk by 40.5 percent in the inter-census period), the Trans-Volga region populated by Volga Germans (population down by 26 percent), and Stalingrad oblast (population down by 18.4 percent). Let us compare these statistics with those of the Azov-Black Sea krai, which was carved out of the North Caucasus: there the rural population declined by 20.8 percent; compare this figure with Ukraine, the population of which shrank by 20.4 percent (Kondrashin 247). Kondrashin depicts the confiscation of food in these epic phrases:

> Under the conditions of the grain deficit, the peasants took advantage of possibilities offered by horticulture, and early in the morning they also headed to the nearest woods to pick mushrooms and berries. These bounties of nature did not eliminate hunger, but they diminished its acuteness and staved off death from starvation. It would appear that they are not subject to state regulation and can be used freely according to designation. But in 1932–33 it was different in the Trans-Volga region and the Don and Kuban regions, just like in other regions of the country... [T]he officials who were in charge of the state grain deliveries, together with the representatives of the village soviet, carried out special raids on the cellars and basements of collective farm members and independent farmers, which were authorized from above.

His final conclusion is as follows:

> Of course, the Party leadership did not sanction the confiscation of all foodstuffs from the pantries and cellars of collective farm members and independent farmers, but the fact that it did not put an end to it in a timely fashion and did not introduce necessary measures to rectify this lawlessness does not free it from responsibility for the deaths of thousands of peasants. (Kondrashin 216, 218)

This is precisely how Kondrashin phrases it: "thousands of peasants." How can this action be characterized as "lawlessness" when the law on fines in kind was in force?

STALIN'S MOTIVES

There was only a brief interval—two and a half weeks—between the New Year's telegram that initiated the terror by famine and the termination of surplus appropriation. Why did these two contradictory actions take place almost at the same time? Perhaps because the terror by famine was a tactical decision and the introduction of the food tax was a strategic one.

In order to understand Stalin's motives, one must view him through the eyes of Soviet citizens of his time. After the victory over the so-called "right-wing deviation," the General Secretary subordinated to himself the top ranks of the Party, Soviet, and Chekist hierarchies of power, but nothing more. The image of the Stalin who was beyond all criticism emerged only after the end of the Great Famine of 1932–33, the Great Terror of 1937–38—with their many millions of victims—and after the Great War [World War II or Patriotic], which, because of him, claimed up to thirty million Soviet citizens. The collapse of state grain deliveries and the All-Union famine of 1932–33 that was directly caused by this failure could have easily cost Stalin his position as General Secretary. Along with this position, control over the top ranks of the governing hierarchies, given the maximized centralization of governance, allowed the General Secretary to do anything he wanted with the citizenry and with it the commune state—anything short of causing a social explosion. The effect of the belated rescinding of the surplus appropriation system could not appear immediately. Meanwhile, the Chekists were signaling that an explosion was indeed brewing. In order not to forfeit his position, the General Secretary put in motion with his New Year's telegram the Chekist operation aimed at the Ukrainian peasantry, which he had begun preparing at the creation of the extraordinary grain delivery commissions.

The analysis of events connected with the progression of the All-Union famine of 1932–33 into various holodomors is based here on Ukrainian materials (with the exception of the Lower Volga krai, where it was necessary to establish famine markers on the basis of material published by Kondrashin). With the aid of these materials, the main goal of my paper is achieved: to prove that the Ukrainian Holodomor, unlike the Holocaust, was the result of certain circumstances coinciding in time and place. The allotted space does not permit an exhaustive examination of this question. However, it is worth formulating several theses concerning aspects of the "shattering blow" that were directly connected with Ukraine.

As emphasized earlier in this article, the USSR was built organizationally on the principles of "democratic centralism," which excluded the emergence of a civil society that might work counter to the commune state. With the multinational composition of the Soviet Union in mind, Bolshevik leaders added to this structure by politicizing ethnicity. Accordingly, already formed nations, including the Russians, reverted to the previous stage of ethnic groups, which precluded the rise of political nations, that is, equivalents of a civil society. Due to the political-administrative and administrative-territorial divisions, the country was a conglomerate of titular ethnic groups that had various rights on the union, oblast, and raion (district) levels. At the same time, representatives of titular ethnic groups outside the limits of their own administrative units were minorities without national rights. The exception was the Russians, who enjoyed unofficial status as the All-Union titular nation and therefore did not feel themselves to be a national minority in any Union or autonomous republic.

Titular nation status demanded the active participation of titular nation representatives ("local people," in Stalinist parlance) in the management of their political-administrative or administrative-territorial unit. As a result, immediately after the formation of the USSR the "indigenization" (*korenizatsiia*) of the government apparatus was launched; in Ukraine this policy was known as "Ukrainization" (*ukrainizatsiia*). The constitutional rights of titular nations turned out to be no more than declarative (as was the right of the Union republics to secede). However, the administrative power of the Soviet organs in all republics, oblasts (or *okruhy*), and raions was full-fledged and thus constituted a threat to the dictatorship, especially in the event of a crisis afflicting the central leadership.

In order to avoid ambiguity in defining a titular nation and its elite and to turn the Kremlin's nationalities policy into an effective instrument of governance, the Soviet leaders included a "fifth heading" indicating nationality, which appeared on forms used for cadre appointments. This changed after the introduction of internal passports in the USSR: a person's nationality was listed under the fourth heading (following surname, given name, and patronymic).

Stalin was apprehensive about Ukraine, a republic whose economic and human resource potential equaled that of all the other national republics combined. The levels of state grain requisitions throughout the regions were set arbitrarily, and we will not be able to substantiate with documents why Ukraine was forced to give the state 7,675,000 tons of grain from the 1930 harvest, while the Central-Black Earth oblast, the Middle Volga krai, the Lower Volga krai, and the North Caucasus krai altogether delivered a total of 7,356,000 tons (Davies and Wheatcroft 470). Neither during the

NEP years nor in the pre-revolutionary period had Ukraine ever produced as much grain as the four highly productive agricultural regions of European Russia taken together. And if we superimpose the state grain delivery statistics onto Lynne Viola's regional statistics of peasant uprisings in 1930 (4,098 in the Ukrainian SSR; 1,373 in Central Black Earth oblast; 1,061 in the North Caucasus; 1,003 in Lower Volga krai, etc. [Viola 138-39]), then it becomes clear that the Kremlin was using the grain procurements as an instrument for punishing the rebellious Ukrainian peasants. At the February–March 1937 plenum of the CC AUCP(B), Stalin, recalling the events of the first months of 1930, when collectivization was halted for half a year, noted: "This was one of the most dangerous periods in the life of our Party" (*Pravda*, 1 April 1937).

In a letter to Kaganovich dated 11 August 1932, the General Secretary expressed his conviction that the half-million-strong CP(B)U harboured "quite a few conscious and unconscious Petliurites, finally—direct agents of Piłsudski" (Khlevniuk 276). He could not know that in 1939 together with Hitler he would swallow Poland, but he remembered the capture of Kyiv by Piłsudski's and Petliura's troops in 1920. That is why Polish-ruled Western Ukraine alarmed him no less than the starving Ukrainian SSR, where a social explosion was brewing. He was similarly alarmed by the third Ukraine—in the North Caucasus krai. The Ukrainization of nearly half the districts of the North Caucasus krai, as emphasized in the CC AUCP(B) resolution of 14 December 1932, titled "Concerning the Course of the State Grain Deliveries in Ukraine, the North Caucasus, and in the Western Oblast," was condemned as "Petliurite" (that is, with statist ambitions) (Rudych and Pyrih 291-94). Stalin struck a "shattering blow" both at the Kuban region and Soviet Ukraine, but in the latter he did not put an end to "Bolshevik," that is, cultural, Ukrainization. Postyshev, dressed in a Ukrainian embroidered shirt, carried that out in Kyiv, the national capital of the Ukrainian people.

The Great Famine eliminated a threat of collapse of the USSR that could have originated with Ukraine. Two generations later, the leading role in this collapse was played not by the Shcherbyts'kyi-led government of Ukraine but by Yeltsin's Russia.

WORKS CITED

Anderson, Kirill, ed. *Stenogrammy zasedanii Politbiuro TsK RKP(b)-VKP(b) 1923–1938 gg.*, 3 vols. Moscow: Rosspen, 2007. Print.

Antipova, O. A., and I. Pigarev, eds. *Golod v SSSR 1930–1934 gg. = Famine in the USSR: 1930–1934*. Moscow: Federal'noe arkhivnoe agenstvo, 2009. Print.

Bukharin, Nikolai. *Izbrannye proizvedeniia*. Moscow: Ekonomia, 1990. Print.

Conquest, Robert. *The Harvest of Sorrow: Soviet Collectivization and the Terror-Famine.* London: Hutchinson, 1986. Print.
Danilov, Viktor, Roberta Manning, and Lynne Viola, eds. *Tragediia sovetskoi derevni: Kollektivizatsiia i raskulachivanie*; Dokumenty i materialy v 5 tomakh, 1927–1939. 5 vols. Moscow: Rosspen, 1999–2006. Print.
Davies, Robert W., and Stephen G. Wheatcroft, *The Years of Hunger: Soviet Agriculture, 1931–1933.* New York: Palgrave Macmillan, 2004. Print.
Devis [Davies], Robert, and Stiven Uitkroft [Stephen Wheatcroft]. *Gody goloda: Sel'skoe khoziaistvo SSSR, 1931–1933.* Moscow: Rosspen, 2011. Print.
Hryshko, Vasyl'. Ukrains'kyi "Holokost", 1933. New York: DOBRUS, 1978. Print.
Ivnitskii, Nikolai. *"Golod 1932–1933 godov: kto vinovat?" Sud'by rossiiskogo krest'ianstva.* Ed. Iurii Afanas'ev. Moscow: RGGU, 1996. Print.
Khlevniuk, Oleg et al., eds. *Stalin i Kaganovich: Perepiska, 1931–1936 gg.* Moscow: Rosspen, 2001. Print.
Klid, Bohdan, and Alexander Motyl, eds. *The Holodomor Reader: A Sourcebook on the Famine of 1932–1933 in Ukraine.* Edmonton–Toronto: Canadian Institute of Ukrainian Studies Press, 2012. Print.
Kuz'mina, L.F., and P.N. Sharova, eds. *Kollektivizatsiia sel'skogo khoziaistva: Vazhneishie postanovleniia Kommunisticheskoi partii i Sovetskogo pravitel'stva, 1927–1935.* Moscow: Izd-vo Akademii nauk SSSR, 1957. Print.
Kondrashin, Viktor. *Golod 1932–1933 godov: tragediia rossiiskoi derevni.* Moscow: Rosspen, 2008. Print.
Kul'chyts'kyi, Stanislav. *Chervonyi vyklyk: Istoriia komunizmu v Ukraini vid ioho narodzhennia do zahybeli, Book 2.* Kyiv: Tempora, 2013. Print.
---. *Holodomor 1932–1933 rr. iak henotsyd: trudnoshchi usvidomlennia.* Kyiv: Nash chas, 2008. Print.
---. "Sozdanie sovetskogo stroia." Istoriia Ukrainy: Nauchno-populiarnye ocherki. Ed., Valerii Smolii. Moscow: OLMA-Media Group, 2008. Print.
Marks, Karl, and Fridrikh Enhel's. *Tvory.* 37 vols. Kyiv: Vydavnytstvo politychnoi literatury, 1958–67. Print.
Mykhailychenko, H., Ie. Shatalina, and Stanislav Kul'chyts'kyi, eds. *Kolektyvizatsiia i holod na Ukraïni, 1929–1933.* Kyiv: Naukova dumka, 1992. Print.
Mytskyk, Iurii. *Ukrains'kyi holokost 1932-1933: Svidchennia tykh, khto vyzhyv.* Kyiv: Vydavnychyi dim "Kyievo-Mohylians'ka Akademiia, 2003–. Print.
Nove, Alec. *An Economic History of the U.S.S.R,* 2nd ed. London: Penguin Books, 1989. Print.
Pravda. 19 February 1933. Print.
Rudych, Feliks, and Ruslan Pyrih, eds. *Holod 1932–1933 rokiv na Ukraïni: ochyma istorykiv, movoiu dokumentiv.* Kyiv: Vydavdytsvo politychnoi literatury Ukrainy, 1990. Print.
Shapoval, Iurii, and Valerii Zolotar'ov. Vsevolod Balyts'kyi. *Osoba, chas, otochennia.* Kyiv: Stylos, 2002. Print.
Stalin, Iosyp. *Tvory.* Vol. 12. Kyiv: Ukrains'ke Vyd-vo Politychnoi Literatury, 1946. Print.
---. *Tvory.* Vol. 13. Kyiv: Ukraïns'ke Vyd-vo Politychnoï Literatury, 1946. Print.
Viola, Lynne. *Peasant Rebels under Stalin: Collectivization and the Culture of Peasant Resistance.* New York: Oxford University Press, 1996. Print.
XVII konferentsiia VKP(b): Stenograficheskii otchet. Moscow: n.p., 1932. Print.

How the Holodomor Can Be Integrated into Our Understanding of Genocide

Norman M. Naimark
Stanford University

Abstract: The study of the Holodomor should be integrated into a broader understanding of genocide as a whole, given that a consensus has evolved among a substantial group of scholars that the Ukrainian Famine of 1932–33 fits the general template of genocide. Raphael Lemkin, who introduced this concept into international legal structures, was clearly aware of the famine in 1932–33 and developed the notion of the "Soviet Genocide in the Ukraine" as a multi-pronged genocidal assault on the Ukrainian people. The events of the Holodomor remained largely unknown to the general Western public until the publication of Robert Conquest's *The Harvest of Sorrow* in 1986. Presently, the links between the study of the Holodomor and genocide studies in North America are relatively underdeveloped. As such, there are many aspects of genocide studies that could be illuminated by an understanding of the Holodomor. These include its examination as a "Communist genocide" as per Mao's 1950s famine or Cambodia, but perhaps more specifically within the context of Stalin's actions in the 1930s. Another important aspect is the problem of isolating ethnic from social and political categories: The Holodomor saw a concomitant attack on the Ukrainian intelligentsia and Ukrainian language and culture. The question of the numbers of victims remains controversial, although the figure of 3 to 5 million Ukrainians who died in Ukraine and the Kuban seems to withstand scrutiny. Finally, there is the question of intentionality. Here, in light of recent interpretations of international law, it seems clear that Stalin was responsible for genocide in the case of the Holodomor.

Keywords: Famine, Genocide, Holodomor, Raphael Lemkin

The study of the Holodomor can and should be integrated into a broader understanding of genocide as a whole. Until recently, arguments among scholars regarding the Ukrainian killer-famine of 1932–33 have focused on *whether* the Holodomor should be considered a case of genocide or not. While it would be premature to conclude that these arguments have been fully resolved, it is nevertheless the case that a consensus has evolved among a substantial group of scholars that the Holodomor fits the general template of genocide.[1] Once one agrees that the Holodomor should be

---

[1] The editors of a recent study of the consequences of the Holodomor note also that there is a growing consensus on the number of victims and on the background and

considered genocide, the issue of how to think about it in the context of the history of genocide as a persistent historical phenomenon becomes particularly salient. How does the Holodomor help us comprehend genocide better and how does examining the Holodomor as genocide help us come to terms in more nuanced ways with the events of 1932–33? The assumption of this essay is that comparing the Holodomor with other episodes of genocide in the modern world and integrating it fully with what we would call "genocide studies" helps illuminate its causes, course, and consequences, as well as the nature of genocide itself.

Raphael Lemkin and the Ukrainian Famine of 1932–33

The appropriate place to begin a consideration of the Holodomor in the context of genocide studies is with the towering figure of Raphael Lemkin, the intriguing and controversial Polish-Jewish lawyer who coined the term genocide, gave it substantial meaning, and helped introduce it into the language and legal structure of the international system. Lemkin was also the founding father of genocide studies, as he researched and drafted large parts of a world history of genocide in the late 1940s and early 1950s. In fact, his contributions to understanding the phenomenon of genocide integrate legal thinking with history and social science in a manner that continues to inspire scholars and students. For our understanding of the Holodomor in the context of genocide, it is important to add that his career also intersected with the history of Ukraine and the Ukrainian Famine, about which he wrote and spoke (Serbyn).

Raphael Lemkin was born in the Białystok region of Poland (then part of the Russian Empire) in 1900.[2] Already in the 1920s in the Polish Second Republic, he was fascinated by such horrific episodes in history as the massacres of the Albigensians in the thirteenth century and the destruction of the Armenians in 1915. Before practicing law in Warsaw, he studied in Lviv, where he surely must have become aware of Ukrainian issues, though to date there is little information on his activities there. In 1933, prompted by the Simele massacre of Assyrian Christians in northern Iraq, Lemkin authored a legal brief sponsored by international lawyers presented to a League of Nations meeting in Madrid that condemned what he called the

---

consequences of the Ukrainian Famine. See Graziosi, Hajda, and Hryn xvi.

[2] Much of the biographical information on Lemkin comes from the most comprehensive scholarly study of his life and work by John Cooper (Cooper) and Samantha Power's groundbreaking book (Power). See also my discussion of Lemkin (Naimark 15–29).

crime of "barbarism." His proposal stated: "Whosoever, out of hatred towards a racial religious or social collectivity, or with a view of the extermination thereof, undertakes a punishable action against the life, bodily integrity, liberty, dignity or economic existence of a person belonging to that collectivity, is liable for the crime of barbarity." Lemkin also introduced to the assembly the concept of "vandalism," the core of which was cultural genocide, the destruction of memorials, churches, language use, and other cultural attributes of groups of people (cited in Power 521, note 6). There are three important aspects of Lemkin's initiatives that need to be emphasized in order to understand the arguments to come: 1) Lemkin identified what was essentially the crime of genocide before the coming of the Holocaust; 2) He included social collectivities into his analysis, perhaps in response to the beginning of Soviet attacks on nationalities; and 3) He understood the linkages between mass killing ("barbarism") and cultural genocide ("vandalism").

Lemkin made little headway with the League of Nations, but with the rise of Nazism in Germany, he became all the more convinced that international law was the only means to insure the rights of groups of potential victims of mass killing. When the Third Reich invaded Poland in September 1939, he found his way out of the country to Sweden and then to the United States, where he taught law at Duke University in 1941. Supported by the Carnegie Endowment for International Peace and serving as a consultant to the War Department in Washington, D.C., Lemkin collected materials on the Axis occupation of Europe, which documented the discrimination against religious and ethnic groups that had become an integral part of Hitler's Europe. In the process, he came up with the term "genocide," which he defined in his 1944 book *Axis Rule in Occupied Europe*: "The practices of extermination of nations and ethnic groups as carried out by the invaders [the Nazis and their allies] is called by the author 'genocide,' a term deriving from the Greek word *genos* and the Latin *cide* (by way of analogy, see homicide, fratricide)" (Lemkin 79). Clearly, Lemkin had found a term that created sparks as it rubbed up against the growing consciousness of the Western public as it eventually confronted the Holocaust and other monstrous crimes of mass killing. Although it was initially hard to arouse much interest in the fate of the Jews during or after the war, Lemkin's experiences with the Nazis and his justifiable fears about what had happened to his family in Poland served to focus much of his efforts on publicizing the desperate plight of the Jews.

An amazingly tireless lobbyist, Lemkin was at Nuremberg in the late fall of 1946, trying to convince the prosecutors to include genocide in the indictment against Nazis standing trial for war crimes. But the international court was much more interested in the condemnation of aggressive war than in the mass murder of the Jews or anyone else. Lemkin then worked the corridors of the United Nations to promote the passage of an international law against genocide. Here he had more success, as the Soviets, Poles, Yugoslavs, and other victims of Hitler's crimes joined forces with Jewish groups to encourage the General Assembly to pass a resolution of December 1946 condemning the crime of genocide "whether it is committed on religious, racial, political, or *any other grounds* [my emphasis]" and charge the U.N. Sixth (Legal) Committee to draft a convention against genocide (Robinson 17-18; see Resolution 96 (I) in appendix 1, 121-22). In the process of the deliberations about the convention, the Soviets and their Allies (and other countries) insisted that social and political groups be dropped completely from the language of the document, which is crucial for thinking about the Holodomor as genocide. Thus, the Convention on the Prevention and Punishment of Genocide, unanimously adopted by the General Assembly of the United Nations on 9 December 1948, with Lemkin in the gallery, famously defined genocide as a variety of "acts committed with the intent to destroy, in whole or in part a national, ethnical, racial or religious group, as such." Although the convention explicitly recognized, in the spirit of Lemkin, that genocide "has inflicted great losses on humanity... at all periods of history," its language and spirit were understandably entwined with the immediate past of world war and the piles of corpses left behind by the Nazis ("The Convention on the Prevention and Punishment of the Crime of Genocide" 38).

Lemkin himself had a fairly clear-headed idea of what the Ukrainian killer famine of 1932-33 entailed. He was well aware of the travails of the Ukrainians under Soviet as well as Nazi rule. He had been deeply suspicious of Soviet power as it spread into Eastern Europe and his native Poland after the Second World War. While in New York, he developed good ties with the exile communities of the so-called "captive nations"—Lithuanians, Latvians, and Ukrainians, among others. In a 1953 speech, called "Soviet Genocide in the Ukraine," Lemkin described the attempted destruction of the Ukrainian nation in four stages: first, the attacks on the Ukrainian intelligentsia, when "teachers, artists, thinkers, political leaders were liquidated, imprisoned, deported"; second, the attack on the Ukrainian churches, priests, and hierarchy, which included the execution of thousands of priests; third, the assault on the villages through an artificial famine—in Lemkin's words "a famine to order, by plan," through excess grain requisitioning; and last, and essential to the entire process, the diminishing and dispersal of the Ukrainian population, while bringing Russians and other nationalities into Ukraine (Serbyn 123-30).

Although Lemkin's instincts about the Holodomor in the 1953 speech were on the mark, he couched his analysis in extreme anti-Soviet and anti-

Communist rhetoric. This fit well with the tenor of Joseph McCarthy's paranoid crusade against Communists in American life, but, at the same, it isolated him from the mainstream of the community of international lawyers. He also displayed in some of his writing an exaggerated Russophobia, though that, too, fit the tenor of the times. The language he used ultimately tended to undermine his attempts to lobby more effectively on behalf of the captive nations. For example, in the speech on "Soviet Genocide in Ukraine," quoted above, he considered the killer famine in the same continuous sequence of historical events as Catherine the Great's persecution of the Crimean Tatars, the mass murders of what he called the "SS troops" of Ivan "the Terrible," the *oprichnina*, the tsarist pogroms against Russian Jews, and "the extermination of National Polish leaders and Ukrainian Catholics by Nicholas I" (Serbyn 123–30). None of these events can be thought of as genocide; none constituted mass killing of the sort represented by the Holodomor. Nevertheless, Lemkin is a real hero of the genocide story, and it is certainly an admirable part of his lasting legacy that he understood the genocidal essence of the 1932-33 killer famine in Ukraine.

Despite Lemkin's best efforts, the Genocide Convention had almost no serious resonance in international affairs until the 1990s, long after his death in relative obscurity in August 1959. The United States Senate would not even ratify the convention until 1986, and the Congress did not accept it into law until 1988. There was also the issue that for nearly forty years after the convention, the definition of genocide and its understanding in Western society was linked almost exclusively to the Holocaust and the fate of the Jews during World War II. It took some time and some effort before scholars and political activists were able to apply the term without opprobrium to other historical cases, like the Armenian massacres of 1915, the Ukrainian Famine of 1932-33, or the elimination of some American Indian tribes.[3]

By the middle of the 1990s, specially appointed international courts began to apply the 1948 Genocide Convention to the crimes of mass murder carried out in Bosnia, Rwanda, Sierra Leone, and eventually Darfur and Cambodia. In international jurisprudence, there was no longer concern that indicting Serb mass murderers like General Ratko Mladić and Radovan Karadžić or convicting the Hutu General Theoneste Bagosora of genocide (and sentencing him to life in prison) diminished in any way the Holocaust.

---

[3] For definitional problems of genocide, see, among others, Levene 35-89 and Weiss-Wendt 42-70.

In fact, the international judges and lawyers sometimes referred in their statements and judgments to the precedents of Nuremberg and to the origins of the Genocide Convention. At the same time, since the mid-1990s the work of the courts—the indictments, the arguments, the witness testimonies, the sentencing—have added measurably to the sophistication of scholarship about genocide, demonstrating again the validity of Lemkin's approach of combining international legal scholarship with historical case studies.[4] Scholars, too, have published increasingly detailed studies about diverse prototypes of genocide that have opened up Lemkin's concept to many previously marginalized cases, including the Holodomor.[5] Perhaps most importantly, genocide has become part of a larger public discourse about international politics; Bosnia, Rwanda, Darfur, and other cases of genocidal mass killing have made front-page news, as Western governments considered whether to intervene, as they are at the moment in Syria. Indicative in some ways of the attention to the issue of genocide is the appointment of Samantha Power as United States Ambassador to the United Nations. Power was one of the first to write comprehensively about genocide and the contributions of Raphael Lemkin.

Although the events of the Holodomor were well known within the Ukrainian community in the United States and Canada almost from the time the horrific starvation was taking place, it took the publication in 1986 of Robert Conquest's much praised—but also earlier much maligned—book *The Harvest of Sorrow* to bring the Holodomor the attention of the broader public (Conquest). (To put this into context, Raul Hilberg had an extremely difficult time trying to publish his foundational *The Destruction of the European Jews*. It came out only in 1961 in English and in 1982 in German! [Hilberg]) It is also worth recalling that scholars frequently criticized Conquest's analysis as storytelling based on unreliable personal memoirs rather than empirically verifiable history. It really took the fall of the Soviet Union and the opening of some Ukrainian and Russian archival collections to domestic and foreign scholars to provide the kinds of data about the Ukrainian countryside and insights into the workings of Stalin's Kremlin that would be convincing to skeptics in and outside of academia.

---

[4] The most successful and useful application of Lemkin's approach is no doubt the international legal scholar William A. Schabas (cf. Schabas).

[5] The most prominent textbooks on genocide include the Holodomor in their considerations: Totten and Parsons (includes a chapter by James Mace); Jones (includes the Holodomor as part of a consideration of Stalin's crimes); Chalk and Jonassohn (includes an excerpt from *Harvest of Sorrow*); and Kiernan.

THE HOLODOMOR AND GENOCIDE STUDIES

At this writing, it is fair to say that the study of the Holodomor is developing very rapidly both in Ukraine and North America and that genocide studies is growing by leaps and bounds. But the links between the two areas of knowledge production are relatively underdeveloped. What follows, then, is an attempt to bridge that gap and to demonstrate that there are many aspects of the study of genocide that are illuminated by an understanding of the Holodomor. At the same time, the Holodomor fits well into the general taxonomy of genocide. It is not an unusual or outlier case, and therefore much can be learned from it. The points enumerated here, it should be clear, are intended as exploratory categories for comparison. These are not meant to be either exhaustive or complete, but rather as starting points for further discussion.

1. Perhaps the most obvious thing to say about the Holodomor is that it is a case of what can be classified as Communist genocide. Communist genocides took place in the Soviet Union in the 1930s, in Maoist China during the Great Leap Forward at the end of the 1950s, and in Cambodia, during the horror years of Khmer Rouge rule, from 1965 to the beginning of 1969. Communism as an ideology in power was susceptible to the transformative millenarianism of charismatic leaders like Stalin, Mao, and Pol Pot. One can read in Marx and especially in Lenin justifications for the elimination of large groups of people for the higher purposes divined by the Communist Party.[6] Violence, in Marx's famous words (according to Engels), is "the midwife of every old society pregnant with a new one" (cited in Fromm 21 from *Das Kapital*, vol. I). But it takes particular kinds of leaders with nearly unlimited power and a complete disdain for human life to engage in the kinds of programs that could take millions of lives without the least hesitancy. This also relates to the disdain of Communist societies for the peasantry. For Mao and Stalin in particular, the peasants were treated as transitional material. Some would argue that Lenin falls into this category of murderers as well. But the differences between Lenin's attitudes towards killing and Stalin's were marked. Lenin's included some rational relationship between means and ends; Stalin's, by most accounts, did not.

2. More specifically, the Holodomor is a case of what might be called "Stalin's genocides" (Naimark 70–79). The Ukrainian killer-famine of 1932–

---

[6] On Lenin, see Pipes 1–11. Pipes notes here that Lenin had an "utter disregard for human life." See as well, Gellately 53–57.

33 fully conformed to the ways in which Stalin constructed a whole series of attacks on alleged enemies of the Soviet Union in the course of the 1930s. There was the murderous de-kulakization campaign in the early 1930s, the attack on nationalities, which stretched from the early 1930s through the war, the elimination of "asocial" groups in Order 00447, and the assault on alleged political conspiracies in 1937–38. Because of their opposition to collectivization and grain requisitioning, the Ukrainian peasants were identified as kulaks (*kurkuls* in Ukrainian), Petliurites, and counter-revolutionaries. Too often in the literature, these events are considered in isolation from one another. Stalin harbored images of a fantastic plot in which the grain delivery crisis, induced by his government's own policies of collectivization, would prompt Polish agents and Ukrainian nationalists to pry the republic loose from the union. "We may lose Ukraine," Stalin ominously wrote to Kaganovich in August 1932.[7] In 1930, just as during the civil war, there were widespread Ukrainian peasant uprisings that could lead to separatist movements. A growing and increasingly sophisticated literature on Stalin emphasizes the role of war scares in the genocidal programs of transformation that he initiated in the 1930s (Khlevniuk 148). In my view—and a study of the Holodomor backs this up—these fantastic plots were fictions that were superimposed on murderous policies of mass killing.

3. The Holodomor was a case of mass killing by starvation. Like Mao's Great Leap Forward, during which, according to Frank Dikötter, 45 million people died, and like Pol Pot's purposeful use of food deprivation to kill alleged opponents from the "new people" (as urbanites, teachers, and other professionals were called by the Khmer Rouge), the Holodomor was brought on by a dictator and his retinue, *not* by natural causes (Dikötter x). The same could be said of Hitler's execution by starvation of nearly three million Soviet POWs in the first years after his invasion of the Soviet Union. Amartya Sen puts the issue of killer famines succinctly when he writes: "... starvation is a matter of some people not *having* enough food to eat and not a matter of there *being* not enough food to eat. While the latter can be a cause of the former, it is clearly one of many possible influences" (Sen 434). We know that in the case of Stalin's Soviet Union, Mao's China, Pol Pot's Cambodia, and Hitler's Germany, there was indeed enough to eat. The cause of death by starvation was purposeful food deprivation. In short, Stalin and the Soviet and Ukrainian Communists with whom he worked took the food

---

[7] Cited in Kuromiya 111–12. An excerpt of the August 11, 1932 letter is reprinted in Klid and Motyl 239–40.

out of the Ukrainian peasantry's mouths; they starved; and they were accorded no succor or relief. They were not allowed to seek food outside Ukraine. Burdened by a newly introduced passport system, they were not allowed after a certain point to travel to cities to find something to eat. Stalin would not admit that there was famine and he forbade foreign relief. All of these aspects of the Ukrainian Famine were, by the by, also characteristic of the Great Leap Forward and Pol Pot's regime.

4. The insights of three memoirs on genocidal starvation, two recently published, one a classic on the Ukrainian Famine, help the reader to understand better the ghastly processes involved. One is a diary by Dawid Sierakowiak, who died in the Łódź ghetto of disease associated with hunger (Sierakowiak). The second is a memoir by Loung Ung, who managed to survive the Cambodian catastrophe, though losing many of her family members, before coming to the United States (Ung). And the third is the memoir of Miron Dolot, *Execution by Hunger*, which was published in 1985. Dolot is a pseudonym for a Ukrainian postwar émigré to the United States, who draws a terrifying picture of rural death in the Cherkasy region of Ukraine in 1932–33. All three accounts have a haunting similarity to them: how people cope with and suffer when confronted with the purposeful deprivation of food; the search for substitutes, which sometimes poison and kill them; the changing body shapes, described as "hour glasses" by Sierokowiak; the same diseases, typhus, dysentery, diarrhea, and edema, which see bodies swell up and ooze liquids.[8] There is the debilitating weakness and subsequent listlessness and the severe challenges to family and morality. I have to say of all the accounts of death in genocide that I have read, death by starvation may be the most painful and heartrending. They are also interchangeable. Accounts of death by hunger, whether in Hitler's ghettos or Stalin's Ukrainian countryside, have a numbing similarity to them. The reports of people going mad with hunger, engaging in cannibalism and necrophagy, are common to genocidal famine situations.[9] Citing the studies of Pitirim Sorokin, Sergei Maksudov writes: "… starvation leads some people to deteriorate, decline, and submit, while other people

---

[8] Sierakowiak 47. Dolot writes, like the others, on the edema: "The bodies of others were swollen, a final stage of starvation. Their faces, arms, legs and stomachs resembled the surfaces of plastic balloons. The tissues would soon crack and burst, resulting in the fast deterioration of their bodies" (Dolot 204–205).

[9] Firsthand accounts of cannibalism and necrophagy in the Ukrainian Famine were available very early on in the two-volume collection *The Black Deeds of the Kremlin: A White Book* (Pidhainy). Thanks to Frank Sysyn for alerting me to the existence of these memoirs.

experience different changes—psychological and emotional; for example, callousness or, even worse, brutality. Prolonged starvation leads to changes in the traditional standards of behavior, and conditioned reflexes of social relations cease functioning.... Starvation begins to define a person's every action, weakening or suppressing the sense of self-preservation and love for one's children and other family members.... Group self-defense weakens and friendly relations disappear; egoism increases; and all sense of humanity disappears" (Maksudov 134). Because governments actively and forcibly deny the victims' desire to seek relief, all hope is lost. The utter indifference to this misery of Stalin, Mao, Pol Pot—of Hitler, Talaat Pasha or the colonial genocidaires of indigenous peoples—is worth registering and seeking to understand.

5. The Holodomor highlights an important problem—even fallacy—in thinking about genocide in exclusively ethnic and national terms, as stipulated in the December 1948 U.N. Convention on the Prevention and Punishment of the Crime of Genocide, the founding document of contemporary jurisprudence—national and international—about genocide. First of all, thinking in terms of ethnic and national identity is often as elusive as identifying class and political groups. One can certainly exaggerate the "constructed" nature of ethnicity or nationality. Still, lines of group identity are always porous, and in genocidal situations, more often than not it is the perpetrators who attribute a particular identity, whether ethnic or national on the one hand or social and political on the other, to the victims, not the victims themselves. Second, many genocides (the Holodomor is only one) have mixed ethnic and class (and/or political) dimensions. And third, there are good reasons to assert that ethnic criteria should not be the sole measure of genocide. Three examples widely separated in time and space will have to suffice to illustrate these points. In the 1980s, the Guatemalan military attacked Mayan highlanders as alleged Communists and as Indians, who were also considered lesser human beings in part because of their lower class status.[10] In short, the perpetrators identified the victims as a mixed social, political, and ethnic group, where one characteristic was almost always assumed by the perpetrators to include the others. A supposed army counterinsurgency against Communist guerillas was simultaneously a murderous attack on impoverished ethnic "others." A second example involves Hitler's T-4 euthanasia program, which killed some 200,000 mentally and physically handicapped Germans, a good number of them children, before the "action" was stopped by

---

[10] On Guatemala, see, among others: Jones 377–411; Schirmer; Sanford.

protests from German relatives and Nazi supporters against the practice (Friedlander). Should not the targeted elimination of a group of one's own people also be considered genocide? The third example has to do with what we commonly refer to as the "Cambodian Genocide." How could it be that in July 2010, the Cambodian prison camp commander and murderer and torturer of as many as 16,000 of his compatriots, Kaing Guek Eav, known as "Duch," was acquitted of all counts of genocide and received a sentence reduced to sixteen years for lesser "crimes against humanity" and "war crimes" because he "only" killed Cambodian urban intellectuals?[11] If he had killed Vietnamese and Cham, as some Khmer Rouge did in very large numbers, though nowhere near the numbers of Cambodians killed, then he could have been convicted of genocide.

The Holodomor and the starvation of the Ukrainian peasantry are also illustrative of the complexity of isolating ethnic from social and political categories. On one level, the Holodomor was an attack on the Ukrainian people (Mace 1–14). It was carried out in the larger context of an attack on the Ukrainian intelligentsia and on Ukrainian language and culture. Yet the abandoning of the Ukrainization (indigenization) campaign—the development of Ukrainian national culture and politics fostered by Moscow in the 1920s—went hand in hand with the attack on Ukrainian peasants in the Holodomor. It was above all the stalwart Ukrainian peasantry that stuck in the craw of the Stalinist leadership, not Ukrainians who lived in Moscow or Siberia, or those who resided in the cities or factory settlements of the Ukrainian Republic. At the same time, the arguments for seeing the Holodomor as an attack primarily on Ukrainian peasantry, a mixed social and ethnic category, should not reduce the case for genocide in the least. The Holodomor resulted from a perfect storm of Stalinist national and peasant policies—which also saw the Ukrainian intellectuals, cultural leaders, and Party members attacked and eliminated. Many thousands were killed or exiled in 1933–34. In 1938 alone, there were 185,000 Ukrainian leaders arrested, the vast majority of whom were shot. An additional 244,000 were deported to the Gulag and special settlements. Stanislav Kul'chyts'kyi writes "…Ukraine was at the epicenter of Stalinist repressions" (Kul'chyts'kyi 9).

6. The question of the number of people who died as a consequence of the Holodomor remains controversial, as the numbers of victims are in almost every case of genocide, though the range in the case of the

---

[11] After a series of appeals by both the prosecution and defense, in February 2012 Duch's sentence was increased to life in prison.

Holodomor has narrowed somewhat with access to the archives. In *Stalin's Genocides*, I refer to 3 to 5 million Ukrainians who died in Ukraine and the Kuban, though there are those who still believe the number is higher and those who think it is lower. Scholars and publicists who seek recognition of a particular genocide from a skeptical audience tend to use higher numbers. Partisans of the victims also tend to inflate numbers, as do those who use genocide as a means to foster national identity. But there are also tendencies in genocide studies that lead to undercounting the number of victims as a way to avoid controversy. This is particularly true of the Armenian genocide, where some Ottomanists will use lower numbers and avoid the word "genocide" altogether in order not to offend the Turkish government or their fellow colleagues.[12] In the case of the Ukrainian Famine, and the Soviet Union, one has to be especially wary of numbers that are produced by the state and by the NKVD. Alexander Yakovlev, who was the first to work systematically in Soviet archives about the repressions of the 1930s, stated flat out that the NKVD systematically underestimated the number of dead (234). Working with census data strikes me as equally problematic. Why should one believe these data any more than one believes Soviet production figures? In Stalinist Russia, numbers were there to be manipulated. At the same time, there is a tendency among scholars who wish to appear unbiased and fair-minded to underestimate the number of victims. If one looks at the use of numbers in Timothy Snyder's estimable *Bloodlands*, almost all of them tend to reflect the lowest estimates (see the appendix "Numbers and Terms" 409–414). Like his unwillingness to use the word genocide to describe the Ukrainian Famine or other cases of Soviet mass killing, his use of low numbers—though, of course, high enough—strikes me as equally untenable as using inflated estimates. For the Ukrainian Famine, for example, he asserts that "3.3 million Soviet citizens (mostly Ukrainians) [were] deliberately starved by their own government in Soviet Ukraine in 1932–33" (411). The number could easily have been much higher. We cannot be sure.

7. Crucial to genocide as a whole, and to analyzing the Holodomor as a case of genocide, is the question of "intent." Here, the international courts, in particular, have helped our understanding of how one should think about intent. First of all, the issue of motivation is not important in assessing intent. We do not need to know why a perpetrator did what he or she did for a genocide indictment, though, of course, the historian is always interested in such questions. We need to know if the perpetrator intended

---

[12] On the dynamics of denial in the Armenian Genocide, see Suny 23–37.

to kill a particular group of victims. One of the constant objections to the argument that the Holodomor was genocide is that it cannot be demonstrated convincingly that Stalin intended to kill the Ukrainian peasants in the famine. There was famine everywhere, the argument goes, and that the Ukrainians were hit as hard as they were resulted from their heavy dependence on agriculture. Nevertheless, there is a growing body of evidence indicating that Stalin indeed intended for Ukrainian peasants in the countryside to die. Most of this evidence is anecdotal, to be sure, but taken altogether, it is convincing about Stalin's intent. Equally important is the way international law has dealt with the question of intent. In two cases having to do with genocide in Srebrenica—Radislav Kristić and Goran Jelisić—and in Jean-Paul Akayesu in connection with Rwanda, the courts determined that genocide can be considered to have taken place even if one cannot establish the chain of command to the very top.[13] This was reaffirmed in the appeals as well as before the International Criminal Court, when Bosnia sued the state of Serbia for genocide. This makes sense historically when dealing with the Holodomor. Stalin was unquestionably in charge of Soviet policy in Ukraine in 1932–33. His deputies implemented that policy. Even if we do not have the kind of systematic evidence as historians that would convince our readers that Stalin ordered the killing of Ukrainians in the countryside by intensifying the harsh conditions of the famine, the events themselves and the context in which they unfolded indicate that he did indeed do so. As a result, Stalin was responsible for genocide in the case of the Holodomor, the Ukrainian killer famine.

WORKS CITED

Akayesu (ICTR-96-4-T). Web. 22 May 2014. <http://www.unictr.org/Portals/0/Case/English/Akayesu/judgement/akay001.pdf>

Chalk, Frank R., and Kurt Jonassohn. *The History and Sociology of Genocide: Analyses and Case Studies.* New Haven: Yale University Press, 1990. Print.

Conquest, Robert. *Harvest of Sorrow: Soviet Collectivization and the Terror-Famine.* New York: Oxford University Press, 1986. Print.

"The Convention on the Prevention and Punishment of the Crime of Genocide." *Totally Unofficial: Raphael Lemkin and the Genocide Convention.* Ed. Adam Strom, et al. Brookline MA: Facing History and Ourselves, 2007. Print.

---

[13] The indictments and judgments can be found online (<www.icty.org>) under: Krstić (IT-98-33) "Srebrenica-Drina Corps"; Jelisić (IT-95-10) "Brčko"; and Akayesu (ICTR-96-4-T).

Cooper, John. *Raphael Lemkin and the Struggle for the Genocide Convention*. New York: Palgrave Macmillan, 2008. Print.

Dikötter, Frank. *Mao's Great Famine: The History of China's Most Devastating Catastrophe 1958–1962*. New York: Walker and Co., 2010. Print.

Dolot, Miron. *Execution by Hunger: The Hidden Holocaust*. New York: W. W. Norton, 1985. Print.

Friedlander, Henry. *The Origins of Nazi Genocide: From Euthanasia to the Final Solution*. Chapel Hill: University of North Carolina Press, 1995. Print.

Fromm, Erich. *Marx's Concept of Man*. London: Continuum, 2004. Print.

Gellately, Robert. *Lenin, Stalin, and Hitler: The Age of Social Catastrophe*. New York: Knopf, 2007. Print.

Graziosi, Andrea, Lubomyr A. Hajda, and Halyna Hryn, eds. *After the Holodomor: The Enduring Impact of the Great Famine on Ukraine*. Cambridge, MA: Harvard Papers in Ukrainian Studies, 2013. Print.

Jelisić (IT-95-10) "Brčko." Web. 22 May 2014. <http://www.icty.org/case/jelisic/4>.

Hilberg, Raul. *The Politics of Memory: The Journey of a Holocaust Historian*. Chicago: Ivan R. Dee, 1996. Print.

Jones, Adam. *Genocide: A Comprehensive Introduction*. 2nd edition. London and New York: Routledge, 2011. Print.

Jones, Susanna. "Guatemala: Genocide and Scorched Earth Counterinsurgency War." *Century of Genocide*. Ed. Samuel Totten and William Parsons. New York: Routledge, 2009. 377-411. Print.

Khlevniuk, Oleg. *The History of the Gulag: From Collectivization to the Great Terror*. Trans. Vadim A. Staklo. New Haven: Yale University Press 2004. Print.

Kiernan, Ben. *Blood and Soil: A World History of Genocide and Extermination from Sparta to Darfur*. New Haven: Yale University Press, 2007. Print.

Klid, Bohdan, and Alexander J. Motyl, eds. *The Holodomor Reader: A Sourcebook on the Famine of 1932–1933 in Ukraine*. Edmonton: Canadian Institute of Ukrainian Studies Press, 2012. Print.

Krstić (IT-98-33) "Srebrenica-Drina Corps." Web. 22 May 2014. <http://www.icty.org/case/krstic/4>

Kul'chyts'kyi, Stanislav. "The Holodomor and Its Consequences in the Ukrainian Countryside." *After the Holodomor: The Enduring Impact of the Great Famine on Ukraine*. Ed. Graziosi, Andrea, Lubomyr A. Hajda, and Halyna Hryn. Cambridge, MA: Harvard Papers in Ukrainian Studies, 2013. 1-13. Print.

Kuromiya, Hiroaki. *Stalin*. Harlow: Longman, 2005. Print.

Lemkin, Raphael. *Axis Rule in Occupied Europe: Laws of Occupation, Analysis of Government Proposals for Redress*. Washington D.C.: Carnegie Endowment for International Peace, 1944. Print.

Levene, Marc. *Genocide in the Age of the Nation State*. Vol. I "The Meaning of Genocide." London: I. B. Tauris, 2008. Print.

Mace, James. "The Man-Made Famine of 1933 in Soviet Ukraine." *Famine in Ukraine, 1932-1933*. Ed. Roman Serbyn and Bohdan Krawchenko. Edmonton: Canadian Institute of Ukrainian Studies, 1986. 1-14. Print.

Maksudov, Sergei. "Dehumanization: The Change in the Moral and Ethical Consciousness of Soviet Citizens as a Result of Collectivization and Famine." *After the Holodomor: The Enduring Impact of the Great Famine on Ukraine*. Ed. Andrea Graziosi, Lubomyr A.

Hajda, and Halyna Hryn. Cambridge, MA: Harvard Papers in Ukrainian Studies, 2013. 123-48. Print.

Naimark, Norman M. *Stalin's Genocides*. Princeton: Princeton University Press, 2010. Print.

Pidhainy, Semen. *The Black Deeds of the Kremlin: A White Book*. Vol. I. Toronto: Ukrainian Association of Victims of Russian Communist Terror, 1953; Vol II. Detroit: Democratic Organization of Ukrainians Formerly Persecuted by the Soviet Regime in U.S.A., 1955. Print.

Pipes, Richard, ed. *The Unknown Lenin: From the Secret Archive*. New Haven: Yale University Press, 1996. Print.

Power, Samantha. *"A Problem from Hell": America and the Age of Genocide*. New York: Basic Books, 2002. Print.

Robinson, Nehemiah. *The Genocide Convention: A Commentary*. New York: Institute of Jewish Affairs, 1960. Print.

Sanford, Victoria. *Buried Secrets: Truth and Human Rights in Guatemala*. New York: Palgrave Macmillan, 2003. Print.

Schabas, William A. *Genocide in International Law: The Crime of Crimes*. Cambridge, England: Cambridge University Press, 2000. Print.

Schirmer, Jennifer. *The Guatemalan Military Project: A Violence Called Democracy*. Philadelphia: Univ. of Pennsylvania Press, 1998. Print.

Sen, Amartya, "Ingredients of Famine Analysis: Availability and Entitlement." *The Quarterly Journal of Economics* 96. 3 (August 1981): 433-64. Print.

Serbyn, Roman, ed. "Lemkin on Genocide of Nations." *Journal of International Criminal Justice* 7 (2009): 123-30. Print.

Snyder, Timothy. *Bloodlands: Europe Between Hitler and Stalin*. New York: Basic Books, 2010. Print.

Suny, Ronald Grigor. "Writing Genocide: The Fate of the Ottoman Armenians." *A Question of Genocide: Armenians and Turks at the End of the Ottoman Empire*. Ed. Ronald Grigor Suny, Fatma Müge Gocek, and Norman M. Naimark. New York: Oxford University Press, 2011. 23–37. Print.

Sierakowiak, Dawid, Alan Adelson, and Kamil Turowski. *The Diary of Dawid Sierakowiak: Five Notebooks from the Łódź Ghetto*. New York: Oxford University Press, 1996. Print.

Totten, Samuel, and William S. Parsons, eds. *Century of Genocide: Critical Essays and Eyewitness Accounts*. New York: Routledge, 2009. Print.

Ung, Loung. *First They Killed My Father: A Daughter of Cambodia Remembers*. New York: HarperCollins, 2000. Print.

Weiss-Wendt, Anton. "Problems in Comparative Genocide Scholarship." *The Historiography of Genocide*. Ed. by Dan Stone. London: Palgrave Macmillan, 2008. 42-70. Print.

Yakovlev, Alexander N. *A Century of Violence in Soviet Russia*. Trans. Anthony Austen. New Haven: Yale University Press, 2002. Print.